# STARTING A NEW LIFE IN PORTUGAL

*The Ultimate Relocating Guide for Nomads*

## Alphonsine Pelletier

# Contents

*Luggage with Portugal's Flag Colors*

I grew up in France, but the first time I went to live abroad, I had no idea of what to expect. I soon found myself alone, in a different time zone, longing for friends and family. I had to acclimate to a new country and learn a new language while trying to find my way around the bureaucracy and the customs. In this book, I am giving you the type of information I wished I was given years ago when I decided to start a new life and find a place I could call home.

Whether you are looking to relocate or for new places to explore, you will find that this travel book is more than a guide; it's a vision of everyday life in Portugal. If you want to enjoy year-round sunny weather, be surrounded by lovely people, and indulge in great food while affording the living costs, then Portugal is the place.

I invite you to turn the page and immerse yourself in what could be your new life. Discover all you need to know about the country, the customs, the bureaucracy, and the locals. Learn about the different visas and pick up a few Portuguese expressions. By the time you reach the last page, you will be booking your trip to one of the most sought-after countries - Portugal.

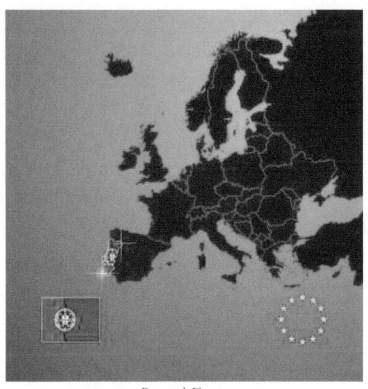

*Portugal, Europe*

# 1

## GETTING TO KNOW PORTUGAL

### "CONHECER PORTUGAL"

You might know that Portugal is in Europe, but did you know that it is also its oldest country? Unbelievable but true! That's because Portugal has had the same borders since 1139. It is geographically in southwestern Europe, by the Atlantic Ocean, on the Iberian Peninsula, a mountainous region also associated with Spain. Since both countries share borders, that means Madrid is only a couple of hours away from the Portuguese capital, Lisbon (or Lisboa as locals call it).

Portugal, today a member of the European Union (EU), was once Europe's greatest power, which explains why there are over 250 million Portuguese speakers around the globe and why Portuguese is the official language of Brazil, Cape Verde, Angola, Guinea Bissau, Mozambique, Principe, Sao Tome, and Equatorial Guinea.

It is also spoken in Goa (India), Macao, and East Timor. People from Portugal and the language of Portugal are both called Portuguese, while anyone with Portuguese descent or origin is called Lusitano/Lusitana or Luso/Lusa for short.

1

Lusitania was an ancient Iberian Roman province located where what is today the country of Portugal.

*"Galo de Barcelos"* (the Rooster of Barcelos) is one of Portugal's emblems, and Lavender is the national flower. Over 80 % of Portuguese people identify as Roman Catholic, even though most consider themselves non-practicing. If you know Portugal because of its seafood dishes, beach destinations, and architecture (Roman and Gothic), you should also know that it is among the world's happiest countries. That is because it is affordable (the currency is the (€) euro), beautiful (you will not get enough of those gorgeous landscapes), friendly (they will welcome you with open arms), and a peaceful country (ranked third in the world in terms of safety).

However, Portugal also produces low-value products such as textiles, clothing, footwear, cork, and paper compared with most Western European Countries. Also, the high levels of bureaucracy have limited entrepreneurship, which may explain why the unemployment rates are so high, resulting in a migration of its youth that has left beautiful villages struggling with depopulation, creating a paradox between the younger generation leaving the country for lack of opportunities and the influx of wealthy immigrants that has resulted in higher costs.

But, as the Minister in the Cabinet of the Prime Minister and for Parliamentary Affairs said: "*Portugal is a country for immigration...A country that wishes to welcome immigrants as it wishes its emigrants to be welcomed, too*".

*Cascais, Portugal*

# 2

## ETIQUETTES RULES AND LOCAL CUSTOMS

### "REGRAS DE ETIQUETA E COSTUMES LOCAIS"

Some people will move to a new country and be disappointed to see that it is not just like home. Having an idea of what to expect when moving to a new country such as Portugal will surely ease your mind and prevent any disenchantment. Below are a few rules and local customs you should be aware of.

Many people keep mistaking Portugal as a province of Spain, which explains why so many Portuguese people get offended when foreigners try to speak Spanish. Still, if you wonder if you can speak Spanish in Portugal, the answer is yes, you can, and most people will even understand you. Just don't be surprised if you get ignored or if they call you out because Portuguese people are polite but also very straight. So, what do you do if you can't speak Portuguese? Try English, even French, or any other language you may know; just avoid Spanish as much as possible.

| **Note:** Portugal is not a province of Spain.

You can get away by speaking any language other than Portuguese because Portugal is a multicultural country. There is an increasing American community mainly living in urban areas because that's where most English-speaking locals are. Other significant communities living in Portugal are Brits, French, Italians, Germans, Russians, Chinese, Brazilians, and Cape Verdeans.

> **Note:** Chances of meeting people who share your culture are high.

It's common to greet strangers in passing in small villages, but not in big cities. The formal way to address an adult, people you are unfamiliar with, or people older than you is to call them "Mister" (*Senhor*) or "Mrs." (*Senhora*) as a sign of respect. This seems especially true for children addressing adults or strangers.

You will use *"Senhora"* for any married or elderly woman. Knowing how to address a person in Portugal will make a difference in how people perceive you, especially if you plan to make long-lasting friendships. So, always greet (*Bom dia,* or *Boa Tarde*) and thank (*Obrigado*) every person you plan on speaking to. Not greeting someone is considered rude, even if you are in a rush. And don't smile or nod in passing. You might think you are being polite; they will think you are bizarre.

> **Note:** There is no gender-neutral expression in Portuguese for non-binary people yet. Portugal still uses traditional male/female pronouns and adjectives only.

A handshake is the most common and appropriate greeting for anyone (men, women, older children). You shake hands with everyone when you get somewhere and do the same when you leave. A man greeting a woman usually waits for the woman to offer her hand before shaking her hand.

However, for an informal introduction to a person, a *"Beijo"* (a kiss) or a *"Beijinho"* (a little kiss) on each cheek is expected from both genders when meeting a woman, starting from the right cheek. Your cheeks may touch, but your lips should not touch the other person's cheek.

It's also common for male relatives to greet each other with a *"Beijo."* Otherwise, men greet one another with a handshake, a hug, or an embrace and may pat each other on the shoulder. They might continue talking while still holding each other's hand and shoulder. Women will shake hands for formal meetings or occasions.

> **Note** to gentlemen: Hands on the woman's shoulders or arms when you greet her with a *"Beijo,"* not the hips.

Extending the thumb, index finger, and pinkie while the other fingers are curled up to form the Devil's Horn is an insult in Portugal. It means cuckold or that your wife/husband or partner is sleeping with someone else.

If you are a woman, avoid going to a bar alone in Portugal if you don't want to attract unsolicited attention. And if you are a businesswoman and need to invite a man to eat for business purposes, go for lunch rather than dinner. If you choose dinner, the polite thing to do is ask the man if he wants to bring his wife/partner along to avoid any misconception.

Other than that, Portugal is a great country for any woman who plans to visit or live in.

Like the rest of Europe, Portuguese people dress nicely when they go out. They are fashion-conscious and see clothes as a symbol of social status and success. So, always dress well and appropriately while in public. Leggings, though acceptable, are seen as too casual. Women would also want to wear comfortable shoes because those cobbled streets might look beautiful in pictures, they date from centuries ago, which means they were not meant to be walked on in high heels or any other uncomfortable shoes.

*Seafood in Cataplana Pan*

If you are invited to dinner and want to bring wine, the safest thing to do is to call your guests and let them know that you were thinking of bringing wine, in which case they might hint at what kind of wine to get. If meat is on the menu, they might be happy to get some extra red wine, for instance. The same goes for perfumes; only gift them if you know which fragrance your host likes. If you choose to bring flowers, count them first. There are 13 of them? Take out one.

Portuguese people are superstitious, and you surely don't want to upset your hosts or anyone around you. Avoid crossing knives, putting the bread upside-down, or leaving a broom behind a door. And when you have to return the invitation, make sure there are not 13 people sitting at the table, as they believe the one with the longest name will die.

But all superstitions aside, table manners are very important in Europe, and Portugal is no exception. It shows that not only do you have class but that you are also educated. So, wait to be shown your seat, and don't start eating until the hostess gives the signal.

You will eat more in Portugal (the food is too good) and later in the evening (think past 8 pm). Strangely enough, you will also get fitter. You will walk a lot unless you have a car or time for public transportation. Once again, beware of those cobblestones; they can become slippery when wet.

And when you eat at a restaurant, drink white wine or "Vinho Verde" (green wine) with seafood, and red wine with meat. Soft drinks are always bottled or canned, so refills are never free. And ask for the check, don't wait for them to bring it to you.

> **Note:** Tipping is totally at your discretion, and you can drink tap water; it is of excellent quality.

9

Public Display of Affection (PDA) is common in Portugal, especially among the younger generation. Kissing a significant other in public has limits, but it is appropriate and not uncommon. Avoid doing it in churches, government buildings, or anywhere you deem unfit.

Portugal passed a law that encourages establishments to ask to see young people's ID when selling them alcohol because there was (and still is) this "tradition" of parents asking their children to go buy them cigarettes or wine. If you find yourself in an establishment that sells cigarettes and alcoholic drinks to minors, there is no need to panic or call child services because no one really cares that much about it.

**Note**: You must be 18 to drink alcohol in Portugal.

Just because you will easily have access to cigarettes and alcohol doesn't mean it goes the same for drugs. Drugs are not decriminalized in Portugal, so don't expect to see people openly selling marijuana or anything illegal. However, possessing small amounts for personal use is not a crime. It will not land you in prison, as you, the consumer (not the dealer), are considered sick and a victim.

**Note**: Portugal is not Amsterdam; purchasing or selling drugs in Portugal is still illegal.

Crime rates are low. Portugal ranks 3rd after Iceland and New Zealand as the safest countries in the world. The government has even made catcalling harassment in the streets a crime. But beware of thieves. Pickpocketing and handbag snatching are common in Portugal, especially in big cities like Lisbon. So, beware of your surroundings; women should hold their purses tight. And don't carry your wallet or cell phone in your back pockets, a sure sign that you are a tourist.

> **Note** to tourists: The thieves won't try to kill or harm you but will do their best to steal your wallet.

Encounters with authorities are less stressful than in America, for instance. The police are usually friendly, and some will even speak English. However, they will take you to the police station if you don't have your Identification Document (ID) or at least a copy. And guns are not allowed without a permit.

> **Note**: Always have your ID or a copy of it (passport, driver's license, residence permit) with you.

Portuguese people are pretty chill and outdoorsy. Not only do they eat and party late (compared to the US, for instance), they won't go to bars before 10 pm, and when the bars close at around 2 AM, they will all head to the nightclubs.

> **Note**: Hanging out in bars and coffee shops is part of the culture.

They will use different words for the same things depending on where you are in Portugal. For example, beer in a glass in Lisbon is called "*Imperial*," but it will be called "*Fino*" in Porto. An espresso (coffee) is "*Bica*" in Lisbon and "*Cimbalino*" in Porto. Or you can say "*Café*," unless you want "*um Galão*" (a coffee with milk) or "*um Abatanado*" (filtered coffee).

> **Note**: Some regions have their own accent and vocabulary.

The Portuguese are football maniacs. Whether you call it soccer or football, *"Futebol,"* your capacity to make new friends might depend on your knowledge of the sport. Cristiano Ronaldo is their number one player and their favorite person.

> **Note**: Do not mistake Cristiano Ronaldo for Ronaldo, the football/soccer player from Brazil.

One of Portugal's national treasures and music pride is called FADO. You will hear it everywhere, from pubs to restaurants to cafés. Just so you know, there are two Fado styles, the Lisbon style - more popular - and the Coimbra style, which is more conservative. How do you differentiate the two? Fado de Coimbra is usually played and sung by men and is more melancholic. The fado played on the radio is usually the Fado of Lisboa. It is more popular and upbeat, which is what the new generation of Fado singers has been playing.

As we mentioned before, Portugal produces low-value products. Now, ever wondered where cork comes from? You will be happy to learn that 50% of the world's cork supply comes from Portugal! It is produced so sustainably that it has minimal impact on the environment!

Lastly, do not criticize Portugal in any aspect as a foreigner. Even if you are surrounded by Portuguese people criticizing their own country, keep it quiet and let them talk. One day, if you become a citizen, you might be allowed to, but until then, you will be a guest.

*Coimbra, Portugal*

# 3

---

## THINGS PEOPLE COMPLAIN THE MOST ABOUT PORTUGAL

### "COISAS DE QUE AS PESSOAS MAIS SE QUEIXAM SOBRE PORTUGAL"

There are around 1.2 million daily smokers in Portugal. In terms of the number of smokers by region, the Azores (23.4%) comes on top, followed by the Alentejo (19.1%) and the Algarve (18.6%). If you are not a smoker, try to avoid picking up the habit. But if you are a smoker, avoid smoking inside commercial establishments, schools, and public buildings. In a word, use your common sense.

Renting a house is far more expensive than buying one in Portugal. However, if you come from a country such as the US, you will find out that even short-term rentals in Portugal are cheaper than in America.

The narrow roads are a fact for most of Europe; nothing specific to Portugal. If you can drive in Portugal, you can do it in any other European country. Also, you must pay a lot for tollbooths or toll roads if you own a car. For your information, the Portuguese are high-speeders. So, if you are a slower driver, just move to the right lane and let them pass you.

If you find the ocean to be too cold, that is because it is the Atlantic Ocean, not the Caribbean. But it will still be less cold than any beach from the French coast and above.

You will soon find out that there are too many tourists in Portugal. Just stay away from big cities like Porto, Lisbon, and Sintra, a must-see on any Portugal itinerary. Also, avoid the famous beaches if possible, and you should be good.

So, the salaries are low, but so is the cost of living. It will all depend on what you do for a living. Life can be difficult if you make the minimum wage, but if you receive something like €2000 or more, your life won't be that bad. That is because Portugal is affordable for people with higher salaries.

Consumer goods are not expensive, and you can order online, but if you are not making enough money, the high housing and energy costs might drain your bank account. And the fact that it is hard to find a well-paid job in Portugal doesn't help either, even if you are qualified. The consequence of that is young people leaving the country for greener pastures. But for those who want to open a business in Portugal, labor is cheap, qualified, and eager to work.

The Portuguese are laid back, and their lifestyle is relaxed. Tardiness, for example, and a last-minute change of plans are all acceptable. Unless you decide to live in Lisbon, you will live in a much slower-paced environment than most Western countries.

They are pretty conservative in their way of thinking too. Very often, you will hear, "That's the way it's always been done" or "Things will eventually get done," which can lead to frustration, especially if you must pay the Portugal Immigration and Border Services, called "*Serviço de Estrangeiros e Fronteiras*" or SEF, or the Department of Health Services (SNS) a visit.

With that relaxed mindset comes bureaucracy which usually translates into long waiting times. They will happily send you back and forth between different departments to do anything. Bring a book or your laptop, and make sure your phone is charged because you will need them to pass the time.

And if the bureaucracy is not enough to complain about, their lunch breaks also tend to be too long. Everything shuts down for lunch for at least 1–2 hours. But fortunately, it is improving. For instance, the Portugal Immigration and Border Services, or SEF, has a pre-booking system that reduces waiting times.

Remember that it gets cold in Europe, and Portugal is no different. Surprisingly, most Portugal houses are not prepared for winter. So, depending on where you live, you might face a gray, damp, cold winter, but the chances of getting snow will be minimal.

I know this is not particular to Portugal, but many people complain about the difficulty of making friends. The sense of not belonging can be hard to overcome, especially when you are new to a country and don't speak the language. That's why it might be a good idea to learn the basics of Portuguese before going there because language can be a barrier for people who find it too difficult to understand.

Technically, it's not that Portuguese is harder to learn; it simply requires more effort! Then, most people speak English, meaning you won't need to be fluent in Portuguese to live in Portugal, especially if you choose to live in Porto or Lisbon. But imagine becoming fluent in the language! What an achievement that will be!

I like to think of the first year of living abroad as the 'honeymoon' phase, where everything is new and exciting. Life usually becomes harder once reality sets in and the feeling of vacationing fades. Anyone who has lived abroad knows this feeling because that is when you start to get nostalgic and miss home the most.

If you can, try to return to your home country at least once a year. This is something to remember when choosing the visa you will apply for to emigrate to Portugal. Having the possibility to travel in the Schengen area or go back home will play a significant role in how much you enjoy living in Portugal.

Remember that making new friends and adjusting to a new country don't happen overnight wherever you go. It takes some time. So, be patient and, most importantly, be open!

> **Note:** If you still see these "cons" as problems, you may not be ready to move to Portugal because integration might be challenging. Otherwise, keep on reading!

*Funicular, Lisbon, Portugal*

# 4

## WHY CHOOSE PORTUGAL?

### "PORQUE ESCOLHER PORTUGAL?"

"Portugal is a safe country" with virtually zero violent crime. You won't risk getting killed. You will have no stress related to personal safety unless you live in some neighborhoods in Lisbon or Porto, where you should be cautious. The only real danger in living in Portugal is sunburn. So, remember to pack that sunscreen!

There is a reason Portugal is known as "one of the best places to retire on Earth." Ask the retirees who live there or look at the number of people applying for the Portugal D7 or Golden Visa, which we discuss in the following chapters, and there will be no doubt left.

Living in Portugal means residing in Europe, which means "easy access to the Schengen Zone." Imagine traveling to France or Spain by car, train, or airplane, spending the weekend, and returning home for work on Monday.

The cold may come as a shock to anyone who has never experienced winter before. Still, you will be glad you moved to Portugal because, winter aside, "the weather is just great," especially for someone looking for a warmer climate. If you want warm weather, go to Portugal!

Did I mention how good "the food" in Portugal is, thanks to their ingredients that are top quality? The country is mainly known for its delicious seafood. And there are more international restaurants now than before, meaning you can pick what and where to eat. And their "Padarias" (bakeries) are simply the best.

"The Portuguese people are conservative and don't accept innovation and significant changes easily," but they are lovely, warm, friendly, and welcoming.

You can't top the quality of life in Portugal. "The cost of living is affordable" compared to most of Europe and the Western world.

And, if you get a residence visa, which we discuss further in the chapters, you will have "access to healthcare for free." However, if you can get Private Insurance, do so. If you can't, no worries; they have you covered.

## FUNNY QUOTES ABOUT PORTUGAL
*"Frases Engraçadas Sobre Portugal"*

- "I love traveling to *Faro*-way places." = I like traveling to faraway places. Faro is the most famous municipality in the Algarve region.
- *"Coim*-bro!" = C'mon, bro! A reference to the city of Coimbra
- "I don't mean to *Braga*, but I look amazing!" = I don't mean to brag, but I look amazing! Braga is a city and municipality in Portugal.

- "It would be a *Sintra* to miss that!" = It would be a sin to miss that! Sintra is the most touristy city in Portugal, not far from Lisbon.

- "I just need someone to *Lisbon* to me." = I just need someone to listen to me!

- "Looking forward to *Tomar*-ow." = Looking forward to tomorrow. Tomar is the last Order of the Knights Templar town in the Santarém district.

- "Do I look *Fatima* in these pants dress?" = Do I look fat in these pants? Fatima is the most visited pilgrimage site in Portugal. Located a 1:30 hour drive north of Lisbon, this is where the Virgin Mary appeared to three shepherd children six times during six months, culminating with the "Miracle of the Sun," where the sun spun in the sky for 10 minutes, leaving the crowd in awe.

- "I crossed a *Porto*-l to another world!" = I crossed a portal to another world! Because drinking too much Porto wine can transport you to another dimension. Unless you were thinking of the city!

Alphonsine Pelletier

*Woman Holding a Fado Guitar*

# 5

## LANGUAGE

### "LINGUA"

Portuguese is the 6th most spoken language in the world and the official language of nine countries. The word *"Portuguese"* refers to the people of Portugal, its language, and its culture. Everyone who is middle class and above in Portugal speaks or can understand English, which means you can still get around if you don't speak Portuguese.

Yet, learning the basics of the language will be a step towards integration in the country because your language proficiency will play a role in how you interact with locals. It will determine your aptitude for participating in conversations and showing interest in their culture.

If you are shy or have difficulties making friends, learning and mastering the language might only open some doors. However, it will help eventually because you will still need it to navigate the local administration.

If you can't afford a private teacher, know that you can still learn the language for free. You must contact your local high schools and ask about the free Portuguese classes offered to foreigners. Another way to learn the language is to exchange with locals. Find people who want to know your tongue and make new friends.

> **Note**: Portuguese from Portugal is usually called European Portuguese in contrast to Brazilian Portuguese.

Portuguese is highly gendered compared to English (and some other languages). It can be hard for new speakers, and it's common for them to make mistakes. Ask to be corrected if you make any mistakes, and don't be offended if they correct you, au contraire, be happy! It is all part of the learning process!

They do not speak Brazilian Portuguese in Portugal, but they understand it. If you speak Brazilian Portuguese, the main difficulty in understanding European Portuguese will be the pronunciation. There are a few phonetic differences between them. European Portuguese has unstressed vowels that make it hard to understand for Brazilians, especially if the person speaking is a fast talker.

There are also differences in vocabulary, but nothing insurmountable, even if it seems to be easier for Portuguese people to understand Brazilians than the other way around. It could be because of the influence of Brazilian music and soap operas (telenovelas) in Portugal. Mozambique and Angola, both in Africa, are the other countries that speak European Portuguese outside of Portugal.

## COMMON EXPRESSIONS IN PORTUGUESE
*"Expressões Comuns Em Português"*

When you learn a new language, the key is to figure out the 100 most frequently used words in that language and start with them. Those words usually make up about 50% of everyday conversations. So, have fun learning new words!

- *"Português"* = Portuguese
- *"Olá"* = Hi! Hello!
- *"Obrigado"* (if you are a male), *"Obrigada"* (if you're a female), regardless of whom you're talking to. = Thank you!
- *"Adeus"* = Goodbye
- *"Bom dia"* = Good morning
- *"Boa tarde"* = Good afternoon
- *"Como vai/vais/está?"* = How are you? How do you do? How is it going?
- *"Bem, obrigado/a! E tu? / E você?"* = Good, thank you. And you? (informal/formal)
- *"Tudo bem?"* = How are you? Is everything fine/okay?
- *"Tudo bem, e consigo(a)?"* = Everything's fine, and you?
- *"Fala/Falas português?"* = Do you speak Portuguese?
- *"Eu falo um pouquinho de português. /Eu falo so un pouco de português "* = I speak a little bit of Portuguese.
- *"Eu não falo muito português."* = I don't speak much Portuguese.
- *"O meu nome é ..."/Eu chamo meu...* = My name is...
- *"Por favor"* = Please

- *"Muito obrigado/a"* = Thank you very much!
- *"De nada"* = You are welcome!
- *"Desculpe"* = Sorry!
- *"Está Bem"/Tá bem"* = It's okay!
- *"Certo"* = Ok (Okay), Right!
- *"Entendido"* = Understood!
- *"De acordo"* = Agreed!
- *"Claro"* = Of course!
- *"É canja"* = Piece of cake, Easy
- *"De/Com certeza/Certamente"* = Sure!
- *"Tranquilo"* = Chill, Low key
- *"Realmente!"* = Really!
- *"A/É sério"* = For real!
- *"Socorro!"* = Help!
- *"Wifi (Uaifai)"* = Wifi
- *"Saúde"* = Cheers!
- *"Vida nova"* = New life
- *"Saída"* = Exit
- *"Bilhete/Senha"* = Ticket

## COMMON WORDS IN PORTUGUESE
*"Vocabulário Comum Em Português"*

Once you know how to pronounce them, they won't sound as foreign, especially if you can speak other Latin languages like French or Spanish.

- *"Cidade"* = City/Town

- *"País"* = Country
- *"Polícia"* = the Police
- *"Estação"* = Station
- *"Rua"* = Street, Road
- *"Avenida"* = Avenue
- *"Autoestrada"* = Highway
- *"Mercado"* = Market
- *"Supermercado"* = Supermaket
- *"Restaurante"* = Restaurant
- *"Centro commercial/Shopping"* = Shopping Center, Mall
- *"Faculdade/Universidade"* = College, University
- *"Escola"* = School
- *"Parque"* = Park
- *"Teatro"* = Theatre
- *"Filho"* = Son
- *"Filha"* = Daughter
- *"Filhos"* = Children
- *"Pais"* = Parents
- *"Familiares/Parentes"* = Relatives
- *"Família"* = Family
- *"Pai"* = Father
- *"Mãe"* = Mother
- *"Deus"* = God

*Restaurant, Alfama, Portugal*

## DATING IN PORTUGUESE
*"Namorar Em Português"*

Dating might not be in your plans when moving to Portugal, but one never knows. In case you meet that special person, here are a few expressions to know.

- *"Namorar"* = to date
- *"Casar"* = to marry, to get married
- *"Namorado/a"* = Boyfriend/Girlfriend
- *"Noivo/Noiva"* = Fiancée (to not be mistaken for *"novio/novia,"* which means boyfriend, girlfriend in Spanish)
- *"Sair com/Andar com"* = To Go out with…
- *"Amar"* = to love
- *"Eu amo-te!"* = I love you! They also say, *"Amo-te."*
- *"Estou apaixonado/a por ti"* = I am in love with you!

30

- *"Tesudo/a"* = Horny

- *"Fofo/a"* = Cute (Can be used for people, animals, children, and objects.)

- *"Eu estou com saudades tuas"* / *"Tenho saudades tuas"* = I am with "saudades" for you! I miss you! I long for you!

- *"Ganhar o coração"* = To win someone's heart

- *"Coração partido"* = A broken heart

- *"Ter sexo"/Fazer amor"* = To make love!

## COMMON SLANG WORDS IN PORTUGUESE
*"Vocabulário De Gírias Comums Em Português"*

When I said that to learn a new language, the key is to figure out the 100 most frequently used words in that language and start with them, well, slang should definitively be among those 100 words. Otherwise, you might never figure out why your plumber keeps saying "Pá."

- *"Fixe"* = Nice, Good, Awesome!

- *"Pá"* = Man! or Dude!

- *"Ya"* = Yeah, Hum!

- *"Giro/Gira"* = Beautiful, Cute, Nice

- *"Tá-se bem"/Tá-se cool=* We are cool; It's all good!

- *"Tipo"* = Like

- *"Desaparece"* = Get lost, Go away

- *"Estou lixado/a"* / *"Lixado/a"* = I am screwed/ I am pissed off (depending on the context).

- *"Baza"* = Easy

- *"Népia"* = Nope

31

Have you ever heard the story of a man visiting a friend in a foreign country who didn't speak the language? He met a girl and asked his friend how to compliment someone in his language. His friend told him a cursing word instead. This might not happen to you but expect to hear many bad words in Portugal because Portuguese people swear a lot. They might be polite people, but they can also be quite vulgar when it comes to cursing. Let's blame their Latin temperament!

## COMMON VERBS IN PORTUGUESE
*"Verbos Comums Em Português"*

The verb conjugation is more complex in Portuguese than it is in English. Portuguese verbs are divided into three conjugation groups: infinitive verbs ending with -ar, -er, and -ir. Try to learn the most used first, regular verbs being the easiest to memorize.

- *"Eu"* = I (me)
- *"Tu"* = You (singular)
- "Você"/ "Vocês" = You (singular)/You (plural, formal)
- *"Ele"*/ *"Ela"* = He/She
- *"Nós"* = We
- *"Eles"*/ *"Elas"* = They (masculine)/They (feminine)
- *"Ser"* = to be (*"Eu sou"* = I am (when talking about something permanent)
- *"Estar"* = to be (*"Eu estou"* = I am (when talking about something temporary)
- *"Querer"* = to want (Eu quero = I want), *"Ter"* = to have

32

- *"Ir"* = to go, *"Vir"* = to come, *"Entrar"* = to enter, to get in, *"Sair"* = to get out

- *"Ver"* = to see, *"Pensar"* = to think

- *"Falar"* = to speak, *"Conversar"* = to talk, *"Dizer"* = to tell (*"Dizer a verdade"* = Tell the truth)

- *"Comprar"* = to buy, *"Vender"* = to sell, *"Pagar"* = to pay

- *"Estudar"* = to study, *"Trabalhar"* = to work

- *"Ligar"* = to call, to telephone, to switch on, *"Sorrir"* = to smile

- *"Fazer"* = to do, to make, *"Construir"* = to build

- *"Pedir"* = to ask, *"Permitir"* = to allow, *"Precisar"* = to need

- *"Tomar"*, *"Levar"* = to take, to carry

- *"Cortar"* = to cut, *"Comer"* = to eat

- *"Trazer"* = to bring, *"Dar"* = to give, *"Pôr"* = to put

- *"Abrir"* = to open, *"Fechar"* = to shut

- *"Andar"* = to walk, *"Correr"* = to run, *"Conduzir"* = to drive

*Algarve Beach, Portugal*

# 6

## MOVING TO PORTUGAL

### "MUDAR-SE PARA PORTUGAL"

#### GENERAL RULES
*"Regras Gerais"*

Covid policies: since July 1$^{st}$, 2022, there have been no requirements for passengers to show proof of vaccination, regardless of their origin or the purpose of the trip to Portugal.

E-visa: In 2020, the Portugal Ministry of Foreign Affairs launched the e-Visa platform. You can now apply for your visa online through the Visa Portal. It is available in five languages: Portuguese, English, French, Ukrainian, and Russian.

When visiting Europe, even for a short period, make sure you have good health insurance covering at least €30,000 in medical and hospital expenses. This also applies to Portugal. You can always make changes once you have settled in the country.

Before applying for a visa, contact your local Portuguese Embassy or Consulate. As well as knowing the procedures, you need to understand how they operate, which can change between consulates. So do not hesitate to call them and ask questions. Also, it is always a good idea to ask a legal representative or consult a law firm if you can afford their fees. They will help you figure out which visa is best for you and help you gather the proper documents, and guide you through the whole process. Remember that having the right documents ready will save you time and money when the time to submit your visa application arrives.

Try to apply at least six months before your intended departure time. If you run out of time, it will be your problem. And make copies of all documents and keep the originals nearby. You will submit them later in the application process. There are cases where you must legalize certain documents, which can be done through an Apostille Stamp or the Portuguese Embassy in your home country. If you need help, call your local embassy and ask questions.

> **Note:** All the documents you provide should be in English or Portuguese. If not, have them translated by a certified translator.

You will need to schedule an appointment at your local embassy/consulate. If you have hired a lawyer, he will take care of everything, and he might accompany you to the appointment where you will submit your documents and attend an in-person interview.

Suppose you are a relative (spouse, dependent child, or parent) or a partner (spouse or legally registered partner) of a European Union (EU) or European Free Trade Association (EFTA) national; you can also move to Portugal under the same rights to live, work, receive education and access social security benefits as your European relative.

> **Note:** EFTA countries are Iceland, Liechtenstein, Norway, and Switzerland.

Remember that you will be deported if you overstay your visa and may be banned from entering the Schengen Zone again for a while, which means if you are banned from Portugal, you will also be banned from the other EU countries.

There are four types of visas: Tourist, Immigration, Student, and Work Visas. Those four types of visas can all fall under these categories: Short Stay, Temporary Stay, and Long Stay Visas, depending on their length and purposes.

A Long Stay or Long-Term Visa is any visa that will last over a year. For example, a Work Visa or Study Visa can be categorized as either a Short-Stay, Temporary, or Long-Stay Visa depending on the length of the visa you need.

In a word, you can get a Long-Stay Visa for work, studies, professional training or internship, or family reunion. Portugal's Golden Visa, D7 Visa, and D2 Entrepreneur Visa fall under the Long Stay Residency Visa category.

*Tavira, Algarve, Portugal*

## MOVING WITH PETS TO PORTUGAL
*"Mudar-Se Com Animais De Estimação Em Portugal"*

Dogs, cats, and ferrets are the only animals allowed in Portugal and must have a microchip linked to a pet passport or a health certificate completed by a veterinarian. Normally, you should have a passport for your pet before traveling to Portugal, but if you need to make one in Portugal, you can get one from any licensed vet. Remember that vet bills are high in Portugal.

Before looking for a pet carrier, make sure your pet receives proper vaccinations, blood tests, and identification microchips. The microchip must be implanted before the rabies vaccination is given.

Some companies will fly your pet to Portugal in a plane cabin. As an alternate insurance policy, buy a flexible flight ticket to fly at the same time/day as your pet in cargo. If your pet can't travel on the date you booked their flight, at least you can change your dates and travel with them.

Portugal is a pet-friendly country, though not as pet friendly as the US, even though pets in Portugal have judicial protection under the law against abuse and negligence. Unjustified animal violence is punishable by imprisonment or fines. You can have only three adult dogs if you live in an apartment in Portugal. That number can go up to 6 with special authorization from a vet.

Your pets can accompany you while using public transportation only if they will cause no trouble. Your small pet should be in a travel kennel wherever you go, while larger dogs must be kept on a leash or muzzle. They also may accompany you into supermarkets or stores that say "pet friendly" on their doors.

And if you are invited somewhere, ask the hosts first if you can bring your pet along, no matter how cute or well-behaved your furry friend is. And if you find someone's pet cute, be courteous and ask first if you can pet them. As a pet owner, you already know from experience that not all dogs or cats like to be touched.

Pets are not allowed on any beach unless it is a designated pet beach, like the North Sand Portinho Beach in Peniche. Until recently, only a few chains, like the Meridien hotel, allowed dogs. Now you can find more pet-friendly places like the

Selina Porto Hotel, where dogs get to stay for an extra fee. Dona Mira Café in Porto is also known to be dog friendly.

There are a few scattered dog parks in big cities. There is a dog park in Vila Nova de Gaia, in Porto. Parque Florestal de Monsanto in Alfama, Lisbon, has dog-friendly trails. There is also a dog park, always in Alfama, that has a fence, some equipment, and water fountains. There is a similar but smaller one in Oeiras, Lisbon, and an even smaller one near Parede, in Cascais. And if you go visit Jardin de Torre de Belem, your furry friend can tag along as long as they are on a leash.

**WHAT YOUR PET NEEDS TO TRAVEL TO PORTUGAL**
*"Requisitos Para O Seu Animal De Estimação Viajar Para Portugal"*

- Identification microchip.
- Proper Vaccination and blood tests.
- Health Certificate issued by an accredited vet.

**INTERNATIONAL MOVING AND SHIPPING COMPANIES**
*"Empresas De Mudanças Transporte Internacionais"*

You should contact international moving and shipping companies to obtain quotes for the transportation of belongings. It is judicious to plan ahead when scheduling your shipment because it may take over a month for your belongings to arrive.

If you are still determining where you will stay when your belongings arrive, make sure they can be properly stored while you are getting settled.

Also, consider the cost comparisons of bringing your belongings by shipping container versus buying everything after you arrive or mailing your packages. For some people, moving to a different country is a way to start over by getting rid of the unnecessary and only keeping the items with sentimental value.

**SHIPPING YOUR CAR**
*"Transportar O Seu Carro"*

Before you ship your car to Portugal, you must have been the owner of that car for over six months by the time of shipping. Just remember that shipping costs have doubled since Covid. If you import your vehicle, remember that it must conform to Portuguese road standards before you can register it.

Also, you will need to have your residence card before you can register your car in Portugal. It might be wiser to sell your car and get a new one in Portugal. If you are afraid to drive a stick shift or manual car, know that electric cars are now pretty standard in Europe.

*Algarve, Portugal*

# 7

## PORTUGAL ENTRY REQUIREMENTS

### "REQUISITOS DE A ENTRADA EM PORTUGAL"

If you are a European Union (EU) or a European Economic Area (EEA) national, you will only need an Identification Document (ID) to enter Portugal. The documents you must present at the Portuguese port of entry depend on your nationality or citizenship.

If you are NOT an EU or an EEA national, you must present a valid passport or travel document and a visa, if applicable, at the Portuguese port of entry.

EEA countries (Iceland, Liechtenstein, and Norway) are not part of the EU but are part of the Single Market Trade (the free movement of goods and people in the EU that allows people to work, shop, travel, study, and retire anywhere in the EU.)

After checking your documents, if the Portuguese Border Officer concludes that you are not a risk for Portugal, you will be permitted to enter the country and thus the Schengen Territory. Make sure that the border officer stamps your passport as a precaution. Without a stamp, you could be fined or detained.

> **Note:** The Border Police hold the final decision if you shall be permitted to enter Portugal or not.

## PAPERWORK
*"Documentação"*

The process of moving to Portugal will prepare you to deal with the country's bureaucracy. But, if you don't want to be bothered by the paperwork and can afford an agent or an immigration lawyer for all the transactions, get one. They will help with the NIF, bank accounts, housing, insurance, schools, translation of documents, the immigration process, and much more.

But first,

## GATHER ALL IMPORTANT DOCUMENTS
*"Réuna Todos Os Documentos Importantes"*

Make sure everything is up to date and you are not missing anything.

- Official Copies of Important Personal Documents for Each Person Traveling
- Official Translations of those documents, if required
- Birth and Marriage Certificates

- Identity Documents (ID): Passport, Identity Card, Driver's license, etc.

- Social Security Cards

- All Vaccinations, Medical, and Dental Records

- Insurance Policies

- Academic Records and Diplomas

- Employment Records

- Proof of Residency (utility bills, bank statements, taxes, etc.)

- A living will if you have one

- Any document you deem necessary

Contact your Portuguese embassy or consulate for information about their requirements. Ask questions about:

- Visas and Permits

- Vaccines for Family Members

- Restrictions or Taxes on Shipped Household Items

- Taxes Involved in Shipping Your Car

- Vaccines and Quarantines for Pets

- Insurance

- Anything you think of or need information about?

## VISAS
*"Vistos"*

Portugal is one of the 27 European countries that are members of the European Union (EU). Portugal is also part of the 26 countries that are members of the Schengen area. The Schengen agreements allow people to travel freely with only a valid passport or an ID card between participating European countries.

> **Note**: Ireland, though a member of the EU, is not a member of the Schengen area, and the United Kingdom (UK) was never a member of the Schengen Area and, since Brexit, is no longer part of the EU.

*Linhares da Beira, Portugal*

## VISA-FREE ENTRY
*"Entrada Sem Necessidade De Visto"*

If you are a Canadian, a US citizen, or are from a country with visa-free agreements with Portugal, or if you have a European Passport and are traveling for reasons such as tourism, family visit, airport transit, business conference, medical reasons, seasonal work, as well as other temporary travel reasons, you won't need a visa to travel to Portugal and the other Schengen Member States for up to 90 days.

> **Note:** Nationals from European countries that aren't Schengen Member States, like Bulgaria, Croatia, Cyprus, Ireland, Romania, and the UK, don't need a visa to enter Portugal either. Still, your passport must be valid for at least six months.

The Schengen Area comprises 22 of the 27 EU Member States plus the four countries that form the EFTA. There are no passport or border controls at the borders within the Schengen Area. The Schengen Member States are Austria, Belgium, Czech Republic, Denmark, Estonia, Finland, France, Germany, Greece, Hungary, Iceland, Italy, Latvia, Lithuania, Luxembourg, Malta, Netherlands, Norway, Poland, Portugal, Slovakia, Slovenia, Spain, Sweden, Switzerland, and Liechtenstein.

> **Note:** Not all European countries are members of the Schengen Area.

Other countries that don't need a visa to travel to Portugal: Australia; Argentina; Brazil; Brunei; Canada; Chile; Colombia; Costa Rica; El Salvador; Ecuador; Guatemala; Israel; Japan; Honduras; Hong Kong; Macau; Malaysia; Mexico; Panama; Paraguay; Peru; New Zealand; Paraguay; San Marino; Seychelles; Singapore; South Korea; Uruguay; the United Arab Emirates and Venezuela.

> **Note:** It's always good to check with the embassy to see if your country is eligible or not for visa-free entry.

Many non-European digital nomads, whose countries have visa-free agreements with Portugal, have taken advantage of this scheme because they could stay in Portugal for 90 days, leave the country, go spend some time in Spain or France, or any other European country, and then come back to Portugal for another 90 days. Those who did that also had to deal with the uncertainty of being admitted back to the country. Also, they risk having worked illegally in Portugal since you cannot work in Portugal with a Visa-Free Stay if you are a non-European Union citizen.

> **Note:** You will be deported if the authorities find out you have been working in Portugal without permission.

## SHORT STAY SCHENGEN VISAS TYPE C
*"Visto Schengen De Curta Duração"*

Schengen Visas are for non-EU citizens traveling for a short period (up to 90 days) to a European Union country and whose countries do not have a visa-free agreement with the Schengen States. This means that your visa might be issued for a shorter period than 90 days or up to 90 days max.

This type of visa can be issued for different purposes, such as tourism, study, work, transit, or family reunion. If you are not a citizen of the country you live in, have a permanent residency card or something similar, and are wondering if you need to pay for a Schengen visa, check with your country of origin to learn about their visa travel agreements with Portugal. Apply for the visa at the Portuguese embassy or consulate in your home country at most six months and within 15 days before your trip to Portugal.

Suppose you are already in Portugal and need to extend your Schengen Visa. In that case, you will need to pay the Portugal Immigration and Border Services, also known as SEF (*Servico de Estrangeiros e Fronteiras*), a visit. Though the chances of it happening might be small, they might comply if you have a valid reason to want your stay extended.

However, you cannot change your tourist visa into a Work Visa while in Portugal, even if you get a job offer during your visit. You must still return to your country of residence or origin and apply to the Portugal Embassy or Consulate for a Work Visa. Once you are approved for the Work Visa, only then will you be able to return and work in Portugal.

There are Subcategories to the Schengen Visa that depend on the reason for travel and the length of stay:

*The Initiation Well, Sintra, Portugal*

## SHORT-STAY TOURIST VISA
*"Visto Turístico De Curta Duração"*

The Short-Stay Tourist Visa allows you to enter the Schengen Area one or multiple times for a maximum of 90 days within 180 consecutive days. This can be the perfect visa for anyone who needs to travel often to Portugal for periods shorter than three months. It is valid between six months to five years and is for nationals whose countries don't have visa-free agreements with Portugal.

Limited Territorial Validity Visa: Depending on the reason for your travel, if there are any restrictions, they will put a sticker on your passport. If SCHENGEN STATES is written on the sticker, then you may travel to all countries within the Schengen Area. But, if one or several country names are listed, you may only visit these countries within the Schengen Area.

Your visa will also state the Number of Entries:

- Single entry means the Schengen visa holder may only enter the Schengen Area once.

- Double entry means the Schengen visa holder may enter and leave the Schengen Area twice.

- Multiple entries mean the Schengen visa holder may enter and leave the Schengen Area as many times as they wish.

Your visa will also specify the Length of Stay. If nothing is specified, the visa will be valid for a maximum of 90 consecutive days (over 180 days) in the Schengen Area. There will be dates indicating the validity of the visa from six months to five years. If your visa states two or more entries, then those dates will determine when you may enter and leave the Schengen Area.

## WHAT YOU NEED FOR SHORT-STAY SCHENGEN VISAS
*"De Que Precisa Para Visto Schengen De Curta Duração"*

- Filled-out Application Forms. (For Minors and Incapacitated People, forms should be signed by the Legal Guardian.)

- 2 Recent Passport Pictures for each applicant

- Valid Passport or Travel Documents plus copies of previous passports and visas, if applicable. The travel document must be valid for at least six months.

- If you are not a national of the country you are applying from, you must show proof that you are Staying Legally in that country; this will be a Green Card for non-US citizens, for instance.

- Travel Reservations. You must show the return ticket if you have already bought your tickets.

- Medical Travel Insurance. If you are getting multiple visas, you will sign a form declaring that you are aware of the need for travel medical insurance for each stay.

- Reasons for Travel or/and Travel Itinerary. Suppose you are traveling for business; they will ask for an invitation stating the purpose of travel and the dates of arrival and departure. If not, bring proof of attendance, registration, or entry ticket to any political, economic, scientific, cultural, sports, or religious events. Or an official document confirming the necessity of the travel if it is for medical reasons.

- Proof of Financial Resources to support you and/or any accompanying family member during your stay, such as work certificates, salary, last three bank statements, etc.

- Travel Authorization for Minors or Court Decision, if applicable

- Proof of Accommodation such as hotel reservations, proof of relationship if staying with family members, or evidence of sufficient finances to cover your accommodation costs. If you will be staying with a Portuguese national or foreign national legally living in Portugal, they can make a statement of responsibility on your behalf.

- Processing Payment Fees

- Some Embassies or Consulates may also request a Criminal Record Certificate.

However, a few categories of people can skip visa fees.

**EXEMPTED FROM SCHENGEN VISA FEES**
*"Isentos Das Taxas Do Visto Schengen"*

- Children under Six Years Old

- Students, Postgraduates, and Teachers traveling for Educational or Training Purposes

- Researchers Traveling for Scientific Purposes

- Representatives of Non-Profit Organizations under 25 years old

- Family Members of EU and EFTA Citizens

## THE AIRPORT TRANSIT VISA
*"Visto De Escala Aeroportuária"*

You usually need the Schengen Transit Visa if your flight makes a stop in Portugal, and you must leave the international transit area and go through police and customs at the airport. If you are a non-EU nomad traveling to another country via Portugal, check with your country of citizenship to see if you need the visa to transit in Portugal, even if you do not leave the transit area. If you are from one of the countries that can enter Portugal without a Schengen Visa, then you can also transit freely, even if you have to leave the airport.

*Porcelain, Fatima, Portugal*

## THE SEASONAL WORK VISA
*"Visto De Curta Duraçao Para Trabalho Sazonal"*

Seasonal workers belong to a sub-category of nomads who frequently travel in need of temporary employment at a particular time of the year. Thus, the Portugal Seasonal Work Visa is for seasonal workers who would work in Portugal for a short period in a specific sector (see below).

It is given for a period equal to or less than 90 days in a field of work previously approved by Portuguese authorities. However, it does not apply to all Schengen Countries but only to the country that issued the visa. Suppose you got your seasonal work visa for Portugal; you can't work in Spain or Greece with it, even if it is in Europe. You must still apply for a Work Visa relating to those countries.

> **Note**: Should you need to stay longer than 90 days, you will need to apply for a Temporary Stay Work Visa.

## LIST OF SECTORS FOR SEASONAL WORK VISA
*"Lista De Setores Para Trabalho Sazonal"*

- Agriculture, Livestock, Hunting, Forestry, and Fishing
- Food, Liquor, and Tobacco Industries
- Instructors (ski, lifeguard, etc.)
- Food Services (Restaurants)
- Gross and Retail Commerce
- Transportation
- Construction
- Freelancers
- Temps

## WHAT YOU NEED FOR A SEASONAL WORK VISA
*"De Que Precisa Para Um Visto De Trabalho Sazonal"*

- Filled-out Petition Application
- Passport or Valid Travel Document
- 2 Recent Passport Pictures
- Return Ticket
- Travel Insurance in case of expatriation or health issues
- If not a national, proof you are living legally in the country where your visa is being issued.
- Proof of Financial Resources to support you and/or any accompanying family member during your stay, such as work certificates, salary, last three bank statements, etc. If you will be staying with a Portuguese national or foreign national legally living in Portugal, they can make a statement of responsibility on your behalf.
- Work Contract or Work Offer (They can also serve as proof of financial resources.)
- Work Accidents Insurance provided by the Employer
- Proof of Accommodation

## THE TEMPORARY STAY VISAS
*"Vistos De Estada Temporária"*

If you need to stay in Portugal for more than 90 days but less than a year and do not want or need to make Portugal your permanent residence, this is the type of visa you need. The Portugal Temporary Stay Visa is Valid for up to 1 year and can be renewed for two years. You can get a Temporary Stay Visa for work, study, training, internship, religious, medical, or youth mobility purposes if you must stay in Portugal longer than three months. You will also be free to travel through the Schengen Area.

The Temporary Stay visa will allow you to work as a self-employed freelancer or an online business owner. Remember that a Temporary Stay visa differs from a Tourist Visa. The deadline for the Portuguese Immigration Authorities to decide on your application is 30 days before your travel date, so it is advisable to start your application ahead of time.

## WHAT YOU NEED FOR A TEMPORARY VISA
*"O Que Precisa Para Um Visto De Estada Temporária"*

You can also find a list of the documents needed at the Ministry of Foreign Affairs of Portugal or your local Portuguese Embassy's official websites.

- Filled-out Application Form. For Minors and Incapacitated People, forms should be signed by the Legal Guardian.

- Valid Passport or Government-issued Travel Document. The travel document must be valid for at least six months.

- Two Recent Passport Pictures for each applicant

- Clean Criminal Records from the country of origin or country of residency (not applicable for minors under 16)

- Health Insurance or Valid Travel Insurance

- If not a national, proof you are living legally in the country where your visa is being issued.

- Proof you can financially support yourself during your stay in Portugal. Bank statements, salaries, etc. If you will be staying with a Portuguese national or foreign national legally living in Portugal, they can make a statement of responsibility on your behalf.

- Form authorizing the Immigration and Border Services (SEF) access to your criminal records

## EXEMPTED FROM TEMPORARY STAY VISA FEES
*"Isentos Das Taxas Do Visto De Estada Temporária"*

- Children under Six

- Family Members of EU and EFTA Citizens living in Portugal

- Students with a scholarship granted by Portugal

- Highly Qualified Researchers

- Patients and Accompanying Persons traveling under Cooperation Agreements in the Field of Health with Portugal

## DIFFERENCES BETWEEN TEMPORARY STAY VISAS AND RESIDENCY STAY VISAS
*"Diferenças Entre Os Vistos De Estada Temporária E Os Vistos De Residência"*

### TEMPORARY STAY VISAS
*"Vistos De Estada Temporária"*

- Valid for more than 90 days but less than a year
- It can be renewed for two-year periods.
- Free travel through the Schengen Area
- All revenue generated should be external to Portugal or online.

### RESIDENCY STAY VISAS OR TYPE D VISAS
*"Vistos De Residência"*

- For stays that last more than one year
- Valid for a 4-month period during which you must apply for a residency permit in Portugal
- The residency permit will be valid for two years and renewable for 3-year periods.
- Free travel through the Schengen Area
- There is a requirement to spend at least 183 days per year in Portugal. You cannot be out of the country for over six or eight non-consecutive months.
- Suitable for a self-employed person or independent workers

*Óbidos, Portugal*

# 8

## THE NOMAD LIFE

"VIDA DE NÓMADA"

In past centuries, nomads traveled as the seasons changed, searching for food or water for their animals. Nowadays, a nomad travels and switches destinations frequently, but contrary to ancient nomads, the modern nomad does not depend on their livestock to make a living.

The nomadic lifestyle has been one of the fastest-growing trends in 2022 because of the pandemic. There are over 15.5 million nomads worldwide, a number that should continue increasing. Today, the word nomadism is an umbrella term that brings together different aspects of the lifestyle.

For instance, nomadic tribalism includes social groups of people who wander around together as a tribe. You will find them in back countries, living off-grid either in their cars, vans, or RVs. Those who go aboard usually travel alone since traveling overseas implies having a passport. And where there is a need for a passport, there will be a need for a visa.

For the longest time, nomads who crossed borders depended on tourist visas to live overseas legally. However, since the

61

tourist visa can only last 30 to 90 days, they lived under a whole scheme that consisted of exiting the country before their visa expiration and spending a couple of days in the nearest country before returning as tourists. Then, everything changed when the Covid 19 Pandemic hit in 2020. With it came the possibility of working remotely, leading to the rise of a new kind of nomadism.

If you are new to the nomadic lifestyle and are unsure if this life is right for you, let's consider the pros and cons of nomadic life to help you make a decision.

## WHY CHOOSE THE NOMAD LIFE?
*"Porque Escolher Uma Vida De Nómada?"*

First, you will get to see the world. Many countries besides Portugal have the Nomad Visa Program. This will also be an opportunity to learn about different cultures and new languages.

Being a nomad, especially a digital nomad, means you will become a Coffee Shop expert. The irony is that it might also become your new office since one of the big perks of becoming a remote worker is no more office hours and no more time spent in traffic going to work.

You can also enjoy summer all year long, depending on which country you choose. The chances for you to feel isolated will be small because there is a vast network of nomads waiting for you.

## WHAT ARE THE CONS OF A NOMAD LIFE
*"Quais São As Desvantagens De Uma Vida De Nómada"*

Unfortunately, there are quite a few cons to nomadic life. One of them is that you will have to learn about visa and tax policies, even if Portugal has a special tax regime for nomads (more on that in the Tax Section).

You might have to use some of your savings if the costs of living end up being higher than what you are making. You must also be resourceful and ready to deal with the unexpected (illness, financial loss, death, inability to renew your visa, and so on).

And one thing often overlooked is that you might become homesick. Being alone and having to make new friends may be a challenge, as well as keeping contact with old ones. The whole nomadic life might prove more complicated than you thought, especially if you must move an entire family. If you are a Digital Nomad, your entire day will depend on Wi-Fi availability, and you will need to adjust your working hours depending on your time zone.

Last but not least, you might not like the country, which happens more often than expected, because there is a huge difference between visiting and living in the so-called country. My advice? Have a plan B.

However, whether you are traveling alone or with a family, are transiting or settling, Portugal has a special spot for you. The country is a mixture of wonders and a hub for nomads, digital nomads, remote workers, retirees, and ex-pats alike. If you are open-minded and ready to do whatever it takes to get accepted by the Portuguese, then you will make friends for life and find a new place to call home.

## FEW WAYS TO MAKE A LIVING AS A NOMAD
*"Algumas Formas De Se Sustentar Como Nómada"*

If you are set on becoming a nomad but are not self-employed and are wondering how to make money while traveling, here are a few ideas to get you started.

- Start a travel blog. Doesn't require any special skills.

- Showcase your photography skills if you have any.

- Are you a web or graphic designer? Time to offer your services.

- Do not disregard waitressing or bartending.

- Never thought of becoming a teacher? Now will be the time. Consider teaching your language as a second language.

- Become a WWOOFer. Don't know what a WWOOFer is? WWOOF, or "Worldwide Opportunities on Organic Farms, is a network that links volunteers to organic farms, where they work on the farm in exchange for food and accommodation."

- How about becoming a Workaway? "A traveler who wants to give back to the communities and places they visit. Open to helping hosts and using the experience to learn and immerse in the local culture." For more information, go to www.workaway.info.

- Go fruit picking. Be a lifeguard, a ski instructor, or a sports coach. This is the time to use your skills and make money while on it.

- Work in a hostel—no strings attached. You can leave whenever you want.

- Sitter; house sitter, babysitter, pet-sitter, garden-sitter. If it needs to be looked after, be that person.

*Ribatejo, Portugal*

# 9

## RESIDENCY VISAS TYPE D

### "VISTOS DE RESIDÊNCIA"

You will need to apply for this type of visa if you are considering staying in Portugal for over a year to become an official resident in Portugal, even if your country has a visa-free travel agreement unless you are an EU or EFTA national. Remember that the visa you get will depend on the duration and the purpose of your stay in Portugal. Several residence visas are available, depending on your income and business activity.

There are two steps to getting your Portugal Residency Visa. You will first need to apply at the Portuguese Embassy in your home country to be issued a double-entry visa valid for four months. Once you have your visa, you will have four months to enter Portugal and book an appointment with SEF (*Serviço de Estrangeiros e Fronteiras*) to get a Residence Permit.

You might get the appointment months away from when you booked it, but don't let that discourage you. Until then, you only need to carry your proof of appointment instead of the permit. You will then renew your residency until the 5-year mark, when you can apply for permanent residence.

Entering Portugal on a D-category visa means you have a Residence Permit from day one and access to everything (free access to other EU countries, schools, and healthcare).

**Note:** With this visa, you must spend at least 183 days per year in Portugal.

## WHAT YOU NEED TO KNOW ABOUT THE RESIDENCY VISAS
*"O Que Precisa De Saber Sobre Os Vistos De Residência"*

- They are valid for four months until you go to Portugal and retrieve your residence permit.

- They give you two entries during those four months.

- Your residence permit will be valid for two years and is renewable.

- Residence Visas differ from Residence Permits. A residence visa will give you the right to travel to Portugal, while the residence permit is the document that will allow you to stay long-term in Portugal.

**Note:** All Long-Term or Residence visas can lead to Portuguese Citizenship.

## PORTUGAL D7 VISA
*"Visto D7"*

The Portugal D7 visa, also known as the Passive Income Visa, was primarily created as a path to residency for non-EEA nationals who wished to settle in Portugal. It was also called the Retirement Visa because that was its first purpose before everyone wanting to live and work in Portugal started using it. Today it is called the Portugal Nomad Visa because of its popularity among nomads and remote workers.

D7 applicants must show that their income or financial investment is at least equivalent, if not twice as much, to the Portuguese minimum wage because, with the rising cost of living in Portugal, the minimum wage typically isn't enough to live comfortably in the major cities. The goal is to show you can live only on your passive income anywhere in Portugal and won't rely on government assistance. To be eligible, you must have at least 12 months' worth of the Portugal minimum wage, plus 50% for the dependent spouse and 30% for the children if you have any.

Remember that the more passive income and savings you can show, the stronger your application will be. Your passive income can come from investment funds, rental income from properties, share dividends, and/or royalties. Depending on the embassy, salaries from remote work outside of Portugal may also make you eligible to apply for the D7 visa.

## WHO CAN APPLY FOR THE D7 VISA
*"Quem Pode Solicitar O Visto D7"*

If you are self-employed, a freelancer, or a remote worker who wants to establish yourself in Portugal, then this is the visa for you. People who wish to retire in Portugal can equally apply for this visa. However, they usually prefer the more popular Golden Visa because they can make their pension, dividends, rental income, or royalties as eligible incomes for this type of visa.

> **Note**: If you want to enter the Portuguese Job Market, you will need to apply for a Portuguese Work Visa.

## WHAT YOU NEED FOR THE PORTUGAL D7 VISA
*"De Que Precisa Para O Visto Português D7"*

You can also find a list of the documents needed at the Ministry of Foreign Affairs of Portugal's official website.

- Completed D7 Application Forms
- Valid Passport or Other Valid Travel Documents
- 2 Recent Passport Pictures
- Travel Ticket
- Health Insurance covering Portugal
- Request for Criminal Records by the Immigration and Border Services (SEF)
- A Cover Letter validating your request
- Proof of Accommodation
- Proof of Financial Support or Sufficient Funds

## APPLICATION PROCESS STEP BY STEP FOR PORTUGAL D7 VISA

*"Processo Passo A Passo Para A Solicitação Do Português Visto D7"*

- First, you will need to fill out the application forms. Make sure all the information matches your travel document.

- Then you will submit your documents and pay the visa fees. You can either mail them or deposit them in person at your local Portuguese Embassy or Consulate. If you have a lawyer, they can assist you with this.

- If your visa application is accepted, you will return to the embassy or consulate to pick up your passport. Your Residency Visa will be in your passport. It will be valid for four months. You are now free to travel to Portugal.

- Once in Portugal, you will make an appointment with SEF (you can call them or make the appointment online) for biometrics to get your Residence Permit. Being in a smaller town will double your chances of getting an early appointment since they are less busy than big cities like Porto or Lisbon.

- It usually takes around two weeks to get your Residency Permit. SEF will notify you when your Residency Permit is ready.

- **Note:** Your Residence Visa allows you to travel to Portugal, while your Residence Permit will allow you to live in Portugal.

## VALIDITY OF A PORTUGAL D7 VISA
*"Validade Do Visto Português D7"*

The D7 visa will give you an initial 2-year validity, after which you can renew it for another three years. To keep your Residency Permit, you must spend over six consecutive months (or 183 days) per year in Portugal or eight non-consecutive months. You can apply for permanent residency or citizenship after five years, which requires proof of integration into society and a language test, for which you will need to have at least the equivalent of a third-grade level or get an A2 language certificate.

## PORTUGAL D2 VISA
*"Visto Português D2"*

The D2 or Business/Entrepreneur Visa is a lesser-known visa than the Golden Visa or the D7 visa. It's called the Business Visa because it implies having a business idea that you can run in Portugal. Your business idea can be anything from a deli shop to a yoga center to a consulting agency. You can also provide services to domestic or international clients.

If you pick the service provider route, you must show proof of having contracts with clients and that you have relevant experience and/or qualifications in your field of work. But the advantage is that being a service provider has fewer requirements than being an entrepreneur since you won't have to incorporate a Portuguese company and won't need an accountant.

Incorporating a company in Portugal implies paying Portuguese Corporation Taxes yearly and making Social Security Contributions. You'll also need to show evidence of having sufficient financial means to set up and run the business.

## WHO CAN APPLY FOR THE D2 VISA
*"Quem Pode Solicitar O Visto D2"*

This visa is intended for non-EU/EEA or Swiss citizens who want to start a new business in Portugal, set up a Portuguese branch of an existing business, or move to Portugal to run a business already here.

In a word, if you are an entrepreneur, freelancer, or independent service provider from outside the EU, EEA, or Switzerland looking to start a new life in Portugal, you might be eligible for a Portugal D2 Visa.

## WHAT YOU NEED FOR THE D2 VISA
*"De Que Precisa Para O Visto D2"*

You can also find a list of the documents needed at the Ministry of Foreign Affairs of Portugal's official website.

- Fill out the D2 form (available on your Portuguese consulate website). Explain in your application why you have chosen Portugal as your business location, why the country would be favorable for you, and how your company will affect Portugal and satisfy the population's needs, like creating multiple jobs or solving a particular issue not yet addressed in the country.

- A Business Plan. You must show that you have set up a company operating in Portugal or have the financial resources to set up a company in Portugal.

- A Portuguese Bank Account

- Proof that funds were transferred to your Portuguese Bank Account from a country other than Portugal

- Show you have enough funds to live without help from the Portugal government.

- A Personal Tax Number

- A Company Registry Number

- A Social Security Number

- Any Employment Contracts

- A Proof of Residence

**Note:** Applying for the D7 visa is more straightforward than the D2 visa.

*Canal, Aveiro, Portugal*

# 10

## THE DIGITAL NOMAD

### "O NÔMADA DIGITAL"

With the Pandemic came the possibility of working remotely. From Bali to Portugal, people were showing up at airports with their most prized possession: their laptops, gaining the nickname of digital nomads because they could work anywhere they wanted as long as their business was accessible online.

Some countries that experienced the influx of that new kind of nomads soon noticed that they were making more money than the locals and therefore buying more expensive goods or services. Witnessing the economic impact of the digital nomads purchasing power, those countries chose to offer them visas appropriately called Digital Nomad Visas, hence normalizing their status.

## WHO ARE THE DIGITAL NOMADS
*"Quien Saos Os Nómadas Digitais"*

Contrary to some beliefs, all digital nomads are not some 20-year-old backpackers traveling the world with their MacBooks. And according to "MBO partners," a business management company, even if 44% of digital nomads are Millennials, 40% are over 36, and some are in their sixties.

The average digital nomad is 32 years old and makes approximately $30,000 annually. There are as many men as women among digital nomads, the majority being White, followed by Hispanics/Latinos, Asians, and Blacks.

So far, the US has gotten the trophy for having the most digital nomads, while Portugal has only 7% of digital nomads worldwide, a percentage that should keep rising. In most cases, digital nomads are called ex-pats, too, just because people can't tell the difference, even if ex-pats are usually tied to a job and a location.

21% of digital nomads work in information technology; 12% in creative services; 11% in education and training; 9% in sales, marketing, and PR; 9% in finance, accounting, and consulting; and 8% in coaching and research.

Even more surprising is that they are reportedly more satisfied with their lives than their non-digital nomad workers counterparts regarding income satisfaction.

## WHERE DO THEY WORK FROM
*"De Onde Trabalham"*

You might have seen them posting on Facebook or Instagram and even envied their lifestyle. But the fact is, since being a digital nomad usually involves no longer having to go to an office, most digital nomads primarily work from their homes, hotel, or hostel rooms.

You can also find them working in coffee shops, coworking spaces, Airbnb, or libraries. Some others will work from their cars, van, or RVs. One setback of this lifestyle is navigating bad Wi-Fi and time zones while trying to meet deadlines.

> **Note:** If you are wondering, Portugal has been listed as the country with the 17th fastest Wi-Fi in the world!

## THE PORTUGAL DIGITAL NOMADS
*"Os Nômades Digitais De Portugal"*

Portugal has become one of the favorite destinations in Europe for digital nomads. Enter any coffee shop or *"Cafetaria"* or *"Café,"* either in Lisbon or Coimbra, and you will find them sitting behind a table (their new office desk), noise-canceling headphones on, and their eyes fixated on their laptops.

Their reasons for choosing Portugal vary. There are a few surfers among them, as Portugal is one of the world's top surf spots and has 364 days of surf! Others are here for the quality of life, "Life is cheaper here," says Ben, who is American and an avid surfer. Others came to Portugal out of curiosity, even though the possibility of working remotely remains the common factor.

## BEST DESTINATIONS IN PORTUGAL FOR DIGITAL NOMADS
*"Os Melhores Destinos Em Portugal Para Nómadas Digitais"*

- As the capital city, Lisbon has become the classic digital nomad city because it provides many services to remote workers. If you are a digital nomad in Portugal, you can't go wrong with Lisbon.

- The second largest city, Porto or Oporto, is rapidly becoming an important choice for digital nomads because of the wide selection of coworking spaces. Old buildings, either downtown Porto or by the beach, have been turned into upscale coworking spaces, giving you access to the best locations and services Porto can offer.

- As Lisbon gets more expensive, many digital nomads have been looking for more affordable alternatives, landing in Costa da Caparica for its proximity to the Portuguese capital.

- The Portuguese upper-class used to spend summer in Sintra, but today it has become a budding international remote worker platform for digital nomads.

- Ericeira is popular with digital nomads because it's an easy 45-minute drive from central Lisbon and is one of Portugal's most popular surf towns.

- The small island of Madeira became one of 2022's hottest digital nomad destinations thanks to the Digital Nomad Village project, launched in 2021 during the Pandemic.

- Lagos is slowly becoming a digital nomad hotspot with new coworking spaces. If you choose to live in downtown Lagos, you will be a few feet away from the beach.

- Artists needing inspiration or those looking to stay away from big cities should head to the beautiful city of Coimbra.

## WHERE TO STAY AS A DIGITAL NOMAD IN PORTUGAL
*"Onde Ficar Em Portugal Como Nómada Digital"*

Even if you plan to settle in Portugal, you might need or want a temporary place to stay once you get there. This will also allow you to get to know the country until you find a place you can call home.

AIRBNB: This is a practical and popular accommodation option for digital nomads in Portugal because of the flexibility in its terms and conditions. You get to choose your stay length without committing to a fixed period.

RENTALS: They can be apartments, homes, or single rooms. What you will pay for rent will depend on which city or town you choose to live in. Not the best option if you are on a budget or if you like the freedom to leave at any time, but perfect for families whose goal is to settle in Portugal eventually. You will need to make a deposit and follow the terms of the lease.

CO-LIVING SPACES: This is a modern form of housing where like-minded people, here digital nomads, share a living space. Other than the apartment or house being rented for a shorter period, it is not that different from having roommates.

81

People have separate bedrooms in co-living spaces and share common areas like living rooms, kitchens, pools, balconies, and bathrooms. The good part is that the chances for you to find someone to share resources, experiences, and skills with will be much higher than just co-habiting with a total stranger. There are two types of co-living spaces, though: static and nomadic. The static co-living spaces have a permanent address. There is no permanent address with nomadic co-living since true nomads move frequently. Besides the web, many real estate agencies specialize in co-living spaces if you are interested in the concept.

HOSTELS: They have been around for so long and are the most budget-friendly accommodation for digital nomads in Portugal. They are also the perfect solution if you are a digital nomad traveling light and constantly on the go.

HOTELS: You can't go wrong with a hotel. However, they are expensive and are unlikely to offer long-term stay options.

## BEST JOBS FOR DIGITAL NOMADS
*"As Melhores Profissões Para Nómadas Digitais"*

- Blogger
- Analyst
- Marketer
- Copywriter
- Podcast Host
- Programmer
- Photographer
- Online Teacher

- Web Developer
- Writer/Journalist
- Creator/Influencer
- Personal Coach or Mentor
- Short Videos Editor
- Content Web or Graphic Designer
- Social Media & Community Manager
- Virtual Assistant.

*Lisbon, Portugal*

# 11

## PORTUGAL DIGITAL NOMAD VISA

"VISTO PORTUGUÊS PARA NÔMADAS DIGITAIS"

So far, the choices given to digital nomads who wanted to stay in Portugal were a tourist visa (you didn't need to open a bank account in Portugal for that, but you could also discover too late that you have been working illegally in a country you were visiting), the Portugal D7 visa, the Portugal D2 visa, and the Portugal Golden Visa.

Over 25 countries have created digital-nomad programs since 2019, with Estonia becoming the first country to offer such a visa. But, On October 30th, 2022, "Portugal positioned itself as a sanctuary for remote workers by launching the PORTUGAL DIGITAL NOMAD VISA, making it available to anyone who makes at least the equivalent of four times the local minimum wage and who wishes to live and work in Portugal."

Many tech companies have remained remote, so tech workers and freelancers have taken advantage of remote-work programs. Now, remote workers from any country that aren't part of the European Union or European Economic Area can apply for the new Portugal Digital Nomad Visa, also called the Remote Work Visa.

The Portugal Digital Nomad Visa will allow individuals and their families to live and work in Portugal legally. It will also give them the right to move freely through the Schengen countries.

Once again, if you're an EU/EEA passport holder, you don't need a Portugal Digital Nomad Visa to work remotely from Portugal. However, declare your presence at the local municipality office (*Camâra Municipal*) and get a Temporary Residency Certificate (usually valid for five years) if you want to stay longer than three months.

## WHO CAN BENEFIT FROM THE PORTUGAL DIGITAL NOMAD VISA
*"Quem Pode Beneficiar Do Visto Português Para Nómadas Digitais"*

- Tech workers
- Writers/Journalist
- Teachers
- Artists
- Business owners
- Freelancers
- Influencers
- Entrepreneurs
- Full-time remote employees
- Anyone who can generate money remotely.

## WHAT YOU NEED FOR THE PORTUGAL DIGITAL NOMAD VISA
*"De Que Precisa Para O Visto Português Para Nómadas Digitais"*

You can also find a list of the documents needed at the Ministry of Foreign Affairs of Portugal's official website. Applicants for the Portugal Digital Nomad Visa and Residence Permit must provide the following:

- Filled out Application Forms. (For Minors and Incapacitated People, forms should be signed by the Legal Guardian.)

- 2 Recent Passport Pictures for each applicant

- Valid Passport or Travel Document. The travel document must be valid for at least six months.

- If not a national, proof you are living legally in the country where your visa is being issued. (This can be a Green Card for non-US citizens).

- Tax Residency Documents

- Proof of income for at least three months (must earn at least four times the equivalent of the Portuguese minimum wage per month)

- For salaried workers, a work contract (the employer must be outside of Portugal) and an annual salary of about $32,760

- For freelancers and self-employed people, job contracts from clients or any other proof of self-employment

You will submit all your documents to either SEF or your local Portuguese Consulate. Those who meet the requirements will apply for a one-year temporary stay visa or a residency permit that can be renewed for up to five years. At that point, you will apply for Permanent Residency or Citizenship.

## PERKS OF PORTUGAL DIGITAL NOMAD VISA
*"Vantagens Do Visto Português Para Nomadas Digitais"*

- You get to live, work and study in a new country.
- Your family (children, spouse, parents) can join you as dependents.
- You can apply for the Non-Habitual Resident (NHR) tax regime.
- You can apply for Portuguese Permanent Residency or Citizenship.
- You can purchase property anywhere if you get a personal fiscal number at the local tax office.
- Once you have all your residency formalities sorted, you will have access to the Portugal healthcare system.

Digital nomads can still apply for Portugal D7 or Portugal Golden Visas. Thus, it is advisable to consider all your choices before deciding which one is best for you, especially if you don't meet all the requirements for the Portugal Digital Nomad. And that's when a lawyer or someone knowledgeable with Portugal immigration services can be crucial.

## DIFFERENCES BETWEEN THE PORTUGAL DIGITAL NOMAD VISA AND THE PORTUGAL D7 VISA
*"Diferenças Entre O Visto Português Para Nómadas Digitais E O Visto D7"*

### PORTUGAL DIGITAL NOMAD VISAS
*"Visto Português Para Nómadas Digitais"*

- Suitable for remote workers
- No need for passive income
- The minimum monthly income must be at least four times the Portuguese minimum wage per month.

### PORTUGAL D7 VISA
*"Visto Português D7"*

- Anyone can apply.
- Earnings must come from passive income.
- Monthly income must equal the Portuguese minimum wage.

*Portuguese Egg Tarts, Portugal*

# 12

## RETIRING IN PORTUGAL

### "REFORMAR-SE EM PORTUGAL"

People over age 65 stopped traveling because of the Pandemic since they were more vulnerable to Covid. But now that the Pandemic is over and retiring abroad has become a possibility again, more and more retirees have been considering Portugal as a potential country to retire to. And this is because "Portugal is for retired people." You will hear that often, which is likely the truth because Portugal is a paradise for retired people with high pensions.

For some, retiring in Portugal will be the opportunity to start a new life, pick up a new skill or put their expertise to work. As for those working remotely, living in Portugal could be an easy transition to retirement. But like any life-changing decision, retiring requires planning. And whether you will retire on a Golden Visa or a D7 visa, there are a few things you still need to know.

For anyone with a small monthly pension, financing real estate or new cars can become complicated once you are over sixty-five in Portugal, and you cannot have an outstanding mortgage balance past the age of seventy-five. If you buy real estate late in life, should you qualify for home financing, your mortgage and your insurance premiums will be much higher.

Also, plan your taxes before moving to Portugal. It is complex and varies according to the source of your income and which country you are from. You'll be classified as a "Non-Habitual Resident," meaning almost no tax on that retirement for the first ten years. If your home country has a double-taxation treaty with Portugal (most Western countries do), you won't get taxed at home, either. Those tax breaks can help you pay for home insulation or gas so that you won't be too cold during winter.

Open a Bank Account before you arrive in Portugal but keep your country address. For instance, it is recommended for Americans living overseas that they maintain a bank account in the States, have their Social Security (SS) checks deposited in the States, then transfer the funds to their bank in Portugal.

For Americans, the American Embassy in Lisbon has a section on direct deposit on SS, and they can answer all your questions. You can also use an International Online Money Transfer App like Wise, which will convert your currency into Euros and wire it to your Portugal bank for very little transaction fees.

Your pensions from any government services - federal, state, local - are exempt from taxes in Portugal. All other sources are taxed (IRA, Roth). However, you will complete your

Portuguese tax return first after you receive your tax assessment, then you will complete your US return and use the Portuguese assessment to calculate your foreign tax credits.

> **Note**: Think of hiring a lawyer or a tax professional if you are not familiar with international laws on taxation.

## PORTUGAL GOLDEN VISA (GV)
*"Visto Gold"*

On February 16, 2023, Portugal's Prime Minister, Antonio Costa, announced the decision to end the program after other European countries, like Ireland, Montenegro, Moldovia, and Cyprus, interrupted their Golden Visa programs.

"Portugal's decision to end the scheme was driven by angst over a surge in house prices that has left many local residents struggling to find adequate accommodation, particularly in Lisbon and Porto, the biggest cities." The Financial Times.

If passed, the law will terminate the Golden Visa by investment in Portugal. But remember that you can still retire in Portugal on a D7 visa (see the chapter about residency visas).

Different countries have different investment options ranging from $250,000 to millions. Even the United States has its Golden Visas, the EB-2 and the EB-5 Investor Visas. This explains why the Golden Visa for Portugal is called the Portugal Golden Visa. It is for non-EU and Swiss nationals who wish to acquire residency in Portugal and eventually Portuguese citizenship.

Of all the countries with a Golden Visa program, the Portugal Golden Visa is one of the most sought-after visas in the world. You wonder why? It grants qualifying investors and their family members (principal applicant, spouse, children under 18 years old, financially dependent children over 18 years old, parents over 65years-old) the right to live, work, and study in Portugal for about five years and travel in Europe as if they were EU citizens.

Also, with a Golden Visa, you can register for Portuguese State Healthcare without paying Social Security Contributions if you choose to live full-time in Portugal. This is possible because it is the Income Tax, rather than the Social Security Contributions, that finances Healthcare.

However, in 2022, the Portuguese government introduced significant changes designed to redirect foreign investment into overlooked regions because people mainly invested in Lisbon (which includes Sintra and Cascais), Porto, some of the Algarve regions, and the coastal towns to obtain a Portugal golden visa. What does that mean? It means you can still buy properties in Portugal with a Golden Visa, but not in those regions since they are no longer eligible for Golden Visa Residential Real Estate Investment.

Only properties in low-density areas, such as the Azores, and the inland territories, are now eligible for the Portuguese Golden Visa. But keep in mind that other areas like Braga can be great investments. Other changes made to the Golden Visa plan include higher minimum investment funds.

> **Note:** some countries like Montenegro, Moldovia, and Cyprus have interrupted their Golden Visa programs.

Golden Visa Processing Fees: During the five years leading to your permanent residence permit, you would pay a one-time Application Fee per person. Add to that the Renewal Application Fees payable each time you renew your resident permit. There are also Government Processing Fees to pay, with dependents like children paying a smaller fee. If you decide to get Portuguese citizenship after six years of legal residency in Portugal, then you should add around €200 for the final Citizenship Fees.

Golden Visa Legal Fees: Even though it's technically possible to complete the whole process on your own, it is such a long and complicated process with large sums of money at stake that most people would rather leave it in the hands of professionals. The legal fees will depend on the law firm and investment types. Count between €5,000 and €10.000 for legal costs for the entire five years. It seems a lot at first, but a lawyer will make the whole bureaucratic application process much easier unless you know what you are doing.

**WHAT YOU NEED FOR A PORTUGAL GOLDEN VISA**
*"O Que Precisa Para O Visto Gold"*

- Open a Bank Account in Portugal
- Transfer Funds to the Bank Account
- Apply for your NIF
- Fill out the Application Forms
- Receipt for Payment of the Application Fees
- Passport Copies for Each Person on your Application

- Declaration from your Portuguese Bank confirming the transfer of funds and stating that they originated outside of Portugal

- Proof of the Portuguese Golden Visa Investment

- Health Insurance covering Portugal

- Certified Criminal Records (from your country of origin or the country you legally reside in)

- Authorization for SEF to check your Portuguese Criminal Records

- Proof from the Portuguese Tax and Customs Authority and Social Security System that you have no Outstanding Debts

- A Signed Declaration stating that you intend to follow the investment requirements

*Alfama, Lisbon, Portugal*

## THERE ARE FIVE TYPES OF INVESTMENTS FOR THE GOLDEN VISA

*"Há Cinco Tipos De Investimentos Quen Podem Proporcionar Um Visto Gold"*

- REAL ESTATE ACQUISITION: Having a house in Portugal has nothing to do with Golden Visa. A property itself won't lead to residency. So, if you want to move to Portugal, you must still apply for a visa, regardless. However, you do not need to live in Portugal to be eligible for this visa.

Once you have made your investment and gotten your visa, you must stay in the country for a minimum of seven days in the first year and 14 days in the following years. You can renew the visa indefinitely as long as you do not sell the investment you got your visa with.

> **Note:** You can purchase real estate with Bitcoin and other cryptocurrencies through intermediaries and qualify for a golden visa.

The amount you will spend acquiring real estate will depend on your finances, needs, and wants. And you must own all the money you invest. A new house in the city will cost more than if it were in a low-density area. And if you buy an old house instead, you can renovate it for even less. You won't pay any property taxes as long as you don't rent it. If you do, expect a 28% flat rate real estate income tax.

The €500,000 Investment Golden Visa Threshold gives you the flexibility to choose any property anywhere in Madeira.

The €350,000 Golden Visa Threshold allows you to invest in a property for rehabilitation/renovation. It includes the property purchase and the value of any rehabilitation work required.

However, the property must be over 30 years old and within one of the official rehabilitation zones defined by each city's local council. This might not be what you had in mind. Still, suppose you consider Funchal, the capital of Madeira, for example. The rehabilitation zone will incorporate a large part of the city's central/downtown area, so if you think outside the box, you can quickly turn your investment into a business.

The rehabilitation of an old property can go from light restoration (minor repairs typically in the bathroom and kitchen) to exceptional, with the new building being of a much higher standard than the old ones.

**Note**: During the rehabilitation process, you should be attentive and considerate of the context and cultural value of the surroundings.

Investing in Low-Density Areas: A further 20% discount is available on Golden Visa property investment thresholds for those investing in low-density areas. That means €400,000 for the regular threshold and €280,000 for the rehabilitation threshold.

**Note**: Madeira is not included in the low-density category.

Property Taxes for Portugal Golden Visa: Residency and Tax Residency are two concepts. With a Golden Visa, you can maintain residency rights without ever becoming a tax resident. However, when buying property anywhere in Portugal, you must pay several taxes, and Portugal taxes real estate heavily.

There are three taxes for property: the Municipal Property Tax (IMI), the Municipal Real Estate Transfer Tax (IMT), and Stamp Duty (IS).

Municipal Property Transfer Tax (IMT): This tax is imposed on real estate transactions. IMT (*Imposto Municipal sober as Transmissões Onerosas de Imóveis*) is calculated either on the tax value of the property or the value declared in the deed of sale; the highest value will prevail. It is payable before buying a property, and its calculation is based on three key factors; the type of property (is it rural or urban), the location of the property (mainland Portugal or autonomous regions like Madeira), and the purpose of the property (primary residence, secondary, business, etc.)

> **Note**: There are a few exemptions to the IMT that a tax specialist can help you figure out and see if your investment is worth it.

The Stamp Duty on Purchase: This tax is imposed on the purchase and sale of a property. The buyer of the house pays this tax when they sign the deed. There's also stamp duty on mortgages, which doesn't apply to Golden Visas. You should consult a Portuguese accountant to see if you are eligible for other reductions.

The Municipal Real Estate Tax (IMI): Unlike the other two, this tax is not payable when you make the purchase but is paid yearly, starting from the moment you buy the property. It's called IMI (*Imposto Municipal Sobre Imóveis*) and will vary depending on the location of your property (a big city or the countryside).

- INVESTMENT FUNDS: Many Golden Visa investors prefer this route, as it's faster and more straightforward than property. You can spend at least €500,000 subscription to a qualifying Portuguese investment fund, also known as *"Fundos de Capital de Risco"* (Venture Capital Fund) or other investment funds that support Portuguese businesses.

  **Note**: You can qualify for any investment options with crypto visa cards.

## BENEFITS OF INVESTMENT FUNDS

- Lower transaction costs, you don't need to pay property taxes.

- They are not taxable in Portugal if you're not a tax resident, a perfect option for an investor who doesn't want to live in Portugal full-time.

- You won't have to worry about expensive property maintenance issues or finding an agency to manage the maintenance for you.

- You won't have to find or manage tenants.

- There is a potentially higher return on the investment when compared to buying property.

- CAPITAL TRANSFER: This is the most expensive option to qualify for a Portugal Golden Visa because it implies making a capital transfer of at least €1.5

million to a Portugal bank account, plus the transfer fees.

- JOB CREATION: There is no minimum amount required to invest. However, you must create at least ten new full-time jobs in a Portuguese business you own or invest in an existing Portuguese business that must create at least five new full-time jobs within three years.

- MAKE A DONATION: You can invest at least €250,000 in preserving national heritage or €500,000 in a research and development activity in Portugal.

## WHY GET A PORTUGAL GOLDEN VISA
*"Porque Obter Um Visto Gold"*

- If you make the required investment and apply for the Portugal Golden Visa, you and your family members will become legal residents of Portugal.

- You can live, work, study, do business, retire, and get access to healthcare in any of the 30 countries in the EU and EEA.

- You will travel in the Schengen area with no visa, though it won't make a big difference for nationals whose countries already have visa-free access to the EU.

- There are little minimum stay requirements: 7 -14 days. Yes, you read that right. By spending seven days per year, you can maintain your residency status and the right to live in Portugal without ever residing there full-time.

- You can benefit from the family reunification program.

- You will get tax benefits. Portugal doesn't tax cryptocurrency gains so you could become a Portugal tax resident and cash out your portfolio. Not only will you generate returns while waiting for your citizenship, but you'll also get your entire investment back upon exit, generally with some capital gains.

- You will become a permanent resident after five years.

- Last, the Golden Visa will give you a Path to Portuguese Citizenship.

## "CONS" OF A GOLDEN VISA
*"Desvantagens De Um Visto Gold"*

- You can't buy anywhere you want. Exit Lisbon, Porto, or the Algarve

- It's a long process that can take up to a year.

- Tax residency is triggered by spending over 183 days in the country.

- It is not instant citizenship by investment program, such as in Malta.

*Cathedral, Faro, Portugal*

# 13

## CITIZENSHIP IN PORTUGAL

### "CIDADANIA PORTUGUESA"

Getting Portuguese citizenship means no more visa restrictions! You will get to vote, work, buy anywhere in Portugal, and travel Europe and the world. You will not have to renounce your citizenship to become Portuguese. Also, you won't have to renounce your citizenship even if you decide not to live in Portugal after all because the country recognizes dual citizenship.

### CITIZENSHIP THROUGH RESIDENCY
*"Cidadania Por Residência"*

After living legally in Portugal for five years, you will be eligible for a Permanent Residence Permit. Permanent residency means you can stay in Portugal if you want, but you won't have rights in the rest of the EU. You can get Portugal citizenship after six years of legal residency. You should at least know basic Portuguese by then.

Try to get an A2 Portuguese Language Certificate on the Common European Framework of Reference for Languages (CEFR) or a *"Certificado Inicial de Português Língua Estrangeira"*

(CIPLE) provided by a *"Centro de Avaliação de Português Lingua Estrangeira"* (CAPLE). Otherwise, your knowledge of the language should be equal to that of a 3$^{rd}$ grade in Portuguese.

You will also need to have a clean criminal record. Golden Visa holders are not subjected to any language requirements to get citizenship. And, once you become a permanent resident or a citizen, you will no longer need to keep your initial investment and will be free to pursue other ventures.

## CITIZENSHIP THROUGH MARRIAGE
*"Cidadania Por Casamento"*

Citizenship through marriage is the easiest and quickest way to acquire Portuguese citizenship. But, if you marry a Portuguese national outside of Portugal, the first step will be to register your marriage at your local consulate, even though some do not handle citizenship applications.

Also, make sure that the marriage is registered in Portugal. You can apply for citizenship after three years of marriage. You will need to provide proof of basic knowledge of the Portuguese language and integration into Portuguese society on top of your birth certificates (yours and your spouse's), a clean criminal record, and your marriage certificate.

If you go to Portugal before getting your citizenship, Register with the *"Junta de Freguesia"* (Parish Council or Board) for a residency certificate (not a visa)

## CITIZENSHIP BASED ON ANCESTRY
*"Cidadania Por Ancestralidade"*

You can claim Portuguese citizenship if one of your grandparents was Portuguese. However, you will need to prove your lineage through legal documents. If you don't have their birth, try going to the Archives of the area where they were born, or check the village where they were born or went to school; maybe there are still traces of them somewhere.

If not, go to the church where they got married if they were Catholics and look into their archives. If the person is dead, the death certificate might indicate their birthplace. Another option is to request their data online.

Also, if you are of Jew Sephardic descent who were expelled from Portugal in the 16th century and can prove it, you may receive Portuguese citizenship.

*Cobbed Street, Lisbon Old Town, Portugal*

# 14

## WORKING IN PORTUGAL

"TRABALHAR EM PORTUGAL"

P ortugal is a haven for digital nomads whose foreign salaries are substantially higher than the average Portuguese salary. However, there are always cases when a person might find themselves in need or want a regular job.

As appealing as nomadism can be, there are some cases where, after a while, a nomad gives up the lifestyle because they find it not to be as fulfilling as they thought or they long for the peace of mind that comes with having a steady 9-5 job. This happens a lot, especially with those who have children or aging parents and have to regularly deal with unexpected events (accidents or illnesses), forcing them to re-evaluate their life choices.

And there are also those who, after spending some time in Portugal and acquiring citizenship or becoming permanent residents, switch careers and take on new opportunities that will give them benefits.

So, no matter your reasons for entering Portugal's job market, here is what you should know.

If you are a professional (doctor, nurse, teacher, etc.) from a foreign country: contact the *"Ordem dos Enfermeiros"* to obtain the equivalence of your diploma. Without this, you cannot practice the profession in Portugal.

If you find a company that can sponsor you for a work visa, great! Once you get a job contract or your work permit is approved, you will need to apply for a Portuguese Work Visa. Or a Residence Permit if you plan to work in Portugal long-term. The type of residence permit you need will depend on your employment.

However, remember that Portugal's local economy and job opportunities are not the best. So, if you want to have a high standard of living, start your own company if you can, which is easy to do in Portugal, and the best part is that it doesn't cost much.

Even better, if you can generate a foreign-based income remotely while living there, do it. Be self-employed or work as a consultant; in all ways, go for a job connected to your passion and natural skills. It is more fulfilling to make a living out of a passion or a learned skill than to do a job you are not interested in.

> **Note:** It is much cheaper to live away from the big cities, but then the salaries also go down.

## WHAT TO EXPECT FROM YOUR EMPLOYER IF YOU FIND A JOB IN PORTUGAL
*"O Que Esparar Do Seu Empregador Caso Encontre Um Emprego Em Portugal"*

## MANDATORY EMPLOYEE BENEFITS
*"Benefícios Obrigatórios Para O Trabalhador"*

- Annual Salaries are divided into 14 payments instead of the standard 12. The extra two salaries are provided as a Christmas bonus paid by the 15th of December and a holiday bonus paid before the employee's annual leave (usually June). Employers need to sign a written agreement with each employee stating when the Christmas and Holiday allowances will be paid.

- Employees in Portugal contributing to social security are covered by basic insurance by the government. This includes healthcare, pension fund, unemployment aid, and paid parental leave.

- Wage Guarantee Fund: Employers must contribute monthly 1% of an employee's gross income to the Working Compensation Fund (*Fundo de Compensação do Trabalho*) and the Working Compensation Warranty Fund (*Fundo de Garantia de Compensação do Trabalho*). This protects employees from the risk of not receiving their salary if the employer defaults.

- Workers Compensation Insurance: All employees must be covered for accidents at work and on the way to and from work.

111

## NON-MANDATORY EMPLOYEE BENEFITS
*"Benefícios Opcionais Para O Trabalhador"*

- Meal Vouchers: It is common to offer employees meal vouchers or lunch cards.

- Public Transportation Allowance: Some companies offer monthly transportation allowance to and from work to employees.

- Supplementary Pension: Some companies offer private pension plans to employees.

- Supplementary Health & Life Insurance: Some employers offer senior-level executives supplementary health and life insurance. Smaller companies usually provide an allowance in place of arranging insurance.

- Commission: Depending on the nature of the job, some employees receive a cash bonus when fulfilling goals, quotas, or targets. The same is valid for seniority bonuses.

- Flexible Working Hours: Most tech companies offer flexible working hours to employees to accommodate their productivity.

- Phone Bills: Some companies offer smartphones to employees and cover the cost of their monthly phone plan.

- Hardware: Tech companies usually allow employees to select their work equipment.

- Business Travel Allowance: For jobs that require business travel, companies usually offer a tax-free daily allowance for trips within Portugal and international trips.

- Gym Membership: Companies in the tech space usually offer gym membership or discounts to their employees.

## HOW TO START A BUSINESS IN PORTUGAL
*"Como Começar Um Negócio Em Portugal"*

Investing in a new business in Portugal is an excellent idea because the country has been attracting many investors. The best cities to start a business are Lisbon and Porto, followed by Cascais, Villa Nova de Gaia, Coimbra, Braga, Sintra, Faro, Leiria, and Funchal.

But before starting a business in Portugal, try to talk to an expert lawyer who knows Portuguese Business Law to help you navigate the process. If you are unfamiliar with the location where you intend to create your business, consider hiring professionals to do marketing research to decide whether it is practicable.

Gather as many documents as possible since you never know what might be needed.

## WHAT YOU NEED TO START A BUSINESS IN PT
*"De Que Precisa Para Começar Um Negócio Em Portugal"*

- A Portuguese Residency Card
- A Personal Tax Number (NIF) from the Portuguese Tax Office.
- A Social Security Number (NISS) from the Portuguese Social Security Office
- A Company's Registry Number
- A well-structured Business Plan

- A Personal and Company Bank Accounts
- Decide on the Business Legal Structure
- Register your business name and address
- Set up your company online or in person
- Start running your business

**Note:** If you are outside Portugal, you should start the application process at your local consulate.

*Douro River, Portugal*

## HIRING A STAFF IN PORTUGAL
*"Contratar Trabalhadores Em Portugal"*

One of the most important aspects for a business to succeed is finding the right employees. Some companies, such as Adecco, Michael Paige, Hays, etc., can assist in the hiring process. Also, there are a lot of online companies that can help if you want to do it yourself.

114

Here are the most relevant costs related to the staff for the employer:

- 14x Salaries per year
- Social Security (11%)
- Employees' vacation period
- Food voucher
- Transportation voucher

> **Note**: It is up to the accountant to conduct the hiring procedure.

## RENTING A SPACE FOR YOUR BUSINESS IN PORTUGAL
*"Arrendar Um Espaço Para O Seu Negócio Em Portugal"*

Renting a place is necessary only if you need a headquarter for your company. The requirements related to where the business is located can vary greatly. Some people would work from home, others from a coworking space or an office. However, you should:

- Provide an address even if you have a digital business
- Decide where the business will be located (inside a shopping center, public space, etc.)
- Carefully analyze your rental agreement to avoid extra costs
- Pay your rent, water, gas, and energy expenses

## REGISTERING YOUR BRAND IN PORTUGAL
*"Registrar A Sua Marca Em Portugal"*

Registering your brand is an optional procedure in Portugal. You do not need it to apply for a Business Visa. You can register at the National Institute of Industrial Property (INPI), but it will require a lawyer to initiate the procedure. After approval, the company can use its brand name without breaking the law.

## FREELANCING IN PORTUGAL
*"Ser Freelancer Em Portugal"*

You can work as a freelancer in Portugal if you have the following:

- A Portuguese Work Visa
- A Residence Permit
- A Tax Number
- A Social Security Number
- And if you make your income tax payments and social security contributions

Many digital nomads are freelancers and might benefit from the Portugal Digital Nomad Visa or the D7 visa. Talk to a representative to see which one is best for you.

## REGISTERING A FOREIGN COMPANY IN PORTUGAL
*"Registrar Uma Empresa Estrangeira Em Portugal"*

To open a branch or subsidiary of your company in Portugal, you will need the following:

- A Portuguese Visa (if you need one)

- Register the Branch Office Name with The Portuguese Institute of Registries and Notary *"Instituto dos Registos e do Notariado"* (IRN)

- Establish and Register the Branch with the Commercial Registry Office

- Show the Parent Company's Incorporation Documents

- A confirmation from the Board of Directors of the parent company confirming the opening of the branch

- A Power of Attorney

> **Note**: If you plan to expand your business to other European countries, having a business in a country that is part of the European Union could be a good start.

*Rabelo Boat, Douro River, Portugal*

# 15

## PORTUGAL WORK VISA

"VISTO DE TRABALHO EM PORTUGAL"

A Portugal Work Visa is the most common work visa for anyone looking to work in Portugal. This is the most commonly used visa for ex-pats.

If you find a company ready to sponsor you for a visa, or if the company you work for has offices in Portugal and sends you there, the Portuguese work visa will allow you to work in Portugal for 1-2 years. You can apply for a Temporary Residency Card after working in Portugal for at least six months. If you wish to work longer than 1 or 2 years, you will need to renew your work permit before it expires.

You will need to reapply for a work permit each time you switch jobs, and your work permit must always match your job position or location. If not, you might get in trouble with the Portuguese authorities. But once you get your permanent residence permit or become a citizen, you won't need to worry about a work visa anymore. You can apply for permanent residence or Portuguese citizenship after working and living in Portugal for five full years.

> **Note:** If you want to apply for a work visa to a European country other than Portugal, consult the consular authorities of that country.

There are two types of work visas: Temporary Stay Visas and Residency Work Visas. These two types of visas differ in validity and allow multiple entries into the country.

The process to get your work visa is done in two steps. Your Employer will first apply for a Work Permit on your behalf from the Portuguese Labor Authorities, and only then will you be able to apply for a Work Visa.

The documents required for your Portugal work visa will be divided into work permit and work visa application requirements.

## HOW TO APPLY FOR A PORTUGUESE WORK VISA
*"Como Solicitar Um Visto Para Trabalhar Em Portugal"*

If you are an EU/EEA or Swiss citizen, you can work in Portugal without acquiring a work visa unless you intend to stay more than three months, in which case you will need to obtain a residency certificate. But, if you are a non-EU citizen, you will need to apply for a spécific work visa relating to your case if you wish to work in Portugal.

Your employer will first need to apply for a Work Permit at the Portuguese Labor Authorities of the Portuguese Immigration and Borders Services (SEF) on your behalf. You will start your Portuguese Work Visa Application once you have received your work permit. You will stay in your country while the visa application is being processed. If you start the process while in Portugal, you will still need to return to your country to retrieve your visa.

Your work visa will grant you entry to Portugal and is only valid for four months. You will need to travel to Portugal within those four months to start the application process for your Residence Permit. You must book an appointment with SEF for biometrics to get the residence permit. The residency permit can be granted for up to 5 years, depending on the work permit type.

You will also need to open a Portuguese Bank Account before applying for your Tax Number (NIF) that you can get before you travel to Portugal. (More on that in the paragraph about Taxes). You will also need to register for social security at the Portuguese Social Security Office.

> **Note**: When applying for your visa at the Embassy, they might make the SEF appointment for you. The Embassy officials require you to explain your departure date and where you will live in Portugal. If you are still determining these, you can schedule your appointment with SEF as soon as you arrive in Portugal.

## REQUIRED DOCUMENTS FOR A PORTUGAL WORK PERMIT
*"Documentos Necessários Para Solicitar Um Visto Para Trabalhar Em Portugal"*

These documents are submitted by your employer and may differ from those required for your Portugal work visa application.

- Portuguese Residence Permit
- Proof of Accommodation in Portugal

- Valid Passport or Government-issued Travel Document
- 2 Recent Passport Pictures
- Criminal Records from your country of residence
- A Work Contract
- Portugal Social Security Number
- Company Tax Statements
- Proof that an EU/EEA or Swiss citizen could not fill the position.

## WHAT YOU NEED FOR A PORTUGAL WORK VISA
*"De Que Precisa Para Um Visto De Trabalhar Em Portugal"*

If you hire a lawyer, he will take care of everything. Depending on the work, some companies will have their lawyers take care of everything on your behalf. You will be requested to provide them with the necessary documents for submission.

- A Filled-out Application Form
- A Passport or Government-issued Travel Document
- 2 Recent Passport Pictures
- Proof you can financially support yourself and any accompanying family members during your stay in Portugal
- Clean Criminal Records
- Health Insurance or Valid Travel Insurance.
- Proof of Accommodation in Portugal
- Employment or Work Contract

- If you are already in Portugal: a visa that proves you legally entered Portugal or proof that you are legally allowed to live in Portugal, such as a Residence Permit or any other relevant visa

## THE PORTUGAL WORK PERMIT VISA PROCESSING TIME
*"Tempo De Processamento De Um Visto Para Trabalhar Em Portugal"*

The Portugal Work Permit processing time will depend on the merit of your visa application. The processing time could be shorter if all the information and documents provided are correct.

Getting your work permit can take anywhere between 60 days to a few months. If you wish to avoid applying for a work permit, there are alternative routes to Portugal Residency.

## VALIDITY OF THE PORTUGAL WORK VISA
*"Validade De Um Visto Para Trabalhar Em Portugal"*

Portugal work visas allow you to work in Portugal for a period exceeding one year. They are the most common visas used for work purposes in Portugal. The validity period will differ depending on your work visa type.

For instance, if you are a seasonal worker or a business traveler and need to be in Portugal for over 90 days but less than a year, you can apply for a Temporary Stay Work Visa, which allows multiple entries during the validity of your visa.

## THE EU-BLUE CARD
*"O Cartão Azul De Ue"*

An EU Blue Card is issued to those who have sought-after skills, and the number of eligible people is fairly small. It doubles as a Portuguese Work Visa and Residency for Highly Qualified Workers from non-EU countries.

It is valid for between 1 and 4 years and allows you to work in 25 of 27 EU member states except for Denmark and Ireland. The main benefit of the EU Blue Card is that once you have it, you won't need to go through the whole visa application again if you decide to find work outside of Portugal, making it much easier to switch jobs.

It also gives the holder access to unemployment benefits for three months and guarantees some other rights (family reunification, etc.) that some national work permits may not offer.

> **Note**: To be eligible for an EU Blue Card, you will need to provide supporting documents that prove your education, skills, and experiences.

## WHAT YOU NEED TO KNOW ABOUT THE EU-BLUE CARD
*"O Que Precisa De Saber Sobre O Cartão Azul Ue"*

- Your country of residence should not be in any of the Schengen member states.

- You will need to provide documents that support your qualification and necessary experiences, such as a University Degree or equivalent qualification.

- You must have a Work Contract or a Job Offer.

- The EU Blue Card does not apply to Self-Employed or Entrepreneurs.

- You must have a High Gross Annual Salary of at least one and a half times the national average of the country.

- Have the necessary Travel Documents and Health Insurance

- To apply, you or your employer must apply in the country where you wish to work

*University of Evora, Portugal*

# 16

## STUDYING IN PORTUGAL

### "ESTUDAR EM PORTUGAL"

As a parent, I know how challenging it is to move with children, no matter their age. And where you move, either a new town or country, will affect your family dynamic. If you are moving to Portugal for work, you won't have much choice about where to live. But if you get to pick where to live, you will probably look for areas with good schools. If your children don't speak Portuguese, look for areas with bilingual or international schools.

### PORTUGAL EDUCATION SYSTEM
*"O Sistema Educativo Em Portugal"*

There are two types of schools in Portugal: public and international. International schools usually teach English. Portugal Public School is free and of relatively high quality. Attending Preschool or *"Jardim de Infância"* is not mandatory in Portugal. However, *"Ensino Basico"* (Elementary School) is mandatory, while *"Ensino Secundario"* (High School) is optional.

Children who don't speak English get to learn with a special teacher assigned to them. The school year starts in September and finishes at the end of June, with breaks for Christmas and Easter. School hours are from around 8.30-9 am to 4-5 pm, depending on the school, with extended care up to 7 pm. Textbooks are free in Primary/Elementary school. Students buy their own books in middle and high school.

Unless they are attending a private school, your child will have no choice but to attend your local school. Elementary or Primary School is divided between *Enseno Básico 1° Cyclo, Enseno Básico 2° Cyclo,* and *Enseno Básico 3° Cyclo.*

## ELEMENTARY/PRIMARY SCHOOL
*"Enseno Básico"*

## Enseno Básico 1° Cyclo"

This is for grades 1 to 4 or children aged 6-10. Children learn Portuguese, Science, Math, and Art lessons at this level.

### ENSENO BÁSICO 2° CYCLO

For grades 5-6 or ages 10-12. More subjects are added to the program: English, Physical Education, History, Geography, Visual Education, and Technology.

### MIDDLE SCHOOL/JUNIOR HIGH SCHOOL

## *"Enseno Básico 3° Cyclo"*

This is for grades 7-9 or ages 13-15. Students get to add a 3rd foreign language to their curriculum. Notice that middle school starts from 7th grade, not 6th, as is usually the case in America.

**HIGH SCHOOL**

## *"Ensino Secundário"*

Students are oriented toward the program that will best fit their interests. They are subject to a final exam at the end of 12th grade. They can also choose between attending college/university or entering the workforce.

> **Note**: Grades are given in numbers, between 1-20, 20 being the highest grade (A) and 10 being the passing grade (C).

**HOMESCHOOLING**
*"Ensino Doméstico"*

It is perfectly legal to homeschool your children in Portugal. Moving to a new country can be a lot to take in, especially for teenagers who have to quickly adapt to a new environment and culture and make new friends.

Some parents whose children come from a school that offers online learning would rather have their children continue their program than start a new one while they are slowly adjusting to the changes. Ex-pats who plan to return home at some point and want their children to be able to pick up where they left off might also opt for this type of program.

However, you still must enroll your child at your local school and get approval from the board before starting your homeschooling program, especially if they are in elementary or middle school.

## SPECIAL NEEDS EDUCATION
*"Necessidades Educativas Especiais"*

Unless your child has extreme needs, in which case they will be sent to a distinctive school; special needs children usually attend regular schools in Portugal.

You should check with your local school and find out what your options are before enrolment. If your child is the first special need for them to have, they might need to review their program and hire a special educator.

For the most part, schools usually have special education teachers who normally follow plans that were crafted to meet the children's needs.

## HOW TO ENROL A CHILD IN A SCHOOL IN PORTUGAL
*"Como Matricular Uma Criança Numa Escola Em Portugal"*

Children must be six before September to be enrolled in a Portuguese public school. Enrollments usually start around May. Check the school website for more information. You will submit your application online and will need the following documents:

- Copies of your and your child's (children's) passports
- Your child's Vaccination Card
- Your Tax Number
- Proof of Residence
- Your child's two recent passport pictures
- If your child attended school before moving to Portugal, get their file from their former school

showing their grades and school level, so your child won't be kept behind.

> **Note**: All the documents must be translated into Portuguese and certified.

## BEST PUBLIC SCHOOLS IN PORTUGAL BY LOCATION
*"As Melhores Escolas Pública Em Portugal De Acordo Com A Localização"*

### COIMBRA

- Escola Secundária Ifanta D Maria
- Escola Secundária José Falcāo

### LISBON

- Escola Basica e Secundária D Filipa de Lencastre
- Escola Secundária de Restelo

### AZORES

- Escola Secundária Manuel de Arriaga

### PORTO

- Escola Basica e Secundária Clara de Resende
- Escola Secundária Garcia de Orta

## VISEU

- Escola Secundária Alves Martins

*Traditional Portuguese Windows*

## BEST PRIVATE SCHOOLS IN PORTUGAL BY LOCATION
*"As Melhores Escolas Privadas Em Portugal De Acordo Com Localização."*

### THE ALGARVE

- Nobel International School Algarve is the oldest private school in southern Portugal. It has over 30 different nationalities of students and teaches both English and Portuguese.

- Vale Verde International School. Students learn both English and Portuguese.

- The German School of Algarve

## LISBON

As the capital city, it makes sense that Lisbon offers a great variety of private and international schools. American schools are harder to find in Portugal compared to British schools. Attending an American school can be a plus for students hoping to attend university in the USA or Canada. However, students who go to British schools can take the International General Certificates of Secondary School (IGCSE), which can be helpful if they attend a British university.

Here is a list of a few schools in Lisbon; check their websites for their annual tuition.

- The British School of Lisbon teaches children ages 2-12.

- The International Christian School of Cascais is an American school located right outside of Lisbon.

- The Carlucci American International School of Lisbon (CAISL) is the oldest American International School. They offer the International Baccalaureate (IB) program and are the only school in Portugal recognized by the US Department of State. It goes from elementary/primary to high school.

- The Lycée Français Charles Lepierre follows the official instructions of France's Ministry of National Education.

- The International Sharing School Taguspark also offers the IB program.

- The German School of Lisbon, also known as Deutsche Schule Lissabon, goes from Kindergarten to Secondary school.

133

**PORTO**

- The International College of Porto (CLIP) is one of the largest international schools in Portugal. They teach both English and Portuguese.

- The Lycée Français International School in Porto

- The Oporto British School (OBS) follows a British curriculum system.

**CASCAIS**

- Greene's Tutorial College, also known as Greene's College Oxford, is in Estoril, a town in the Municipality of Cascais. Every student has a Personal Tutor. Most courses are delivered to students aged 14-18 individually or in small groups. They follow the British curriculum.

- St. Dominic's International School in São Domingos de Rana is a parish in the municipality of Cascais. It is the only school in Portugal authorized to offer all three programs of the International Baccalaureate.

## UNIVERSITIES IN PORTUGAL
*"Universidades Em Portugal"*

Portugal has been attracting international students because the cost of tuition and living in Portugal is low compared to other European countries. If you need to work while attending college, know that as an international student from a non-EU country, you can work up to 20 hours per week part-time during the school year or full-time during school breaks.

Before you start the job, you will need to be approved by SEF. There are private and government-funded scholarships available to EU and non-EU students. Check the availability and eligibility criteria if you are interested.

## UNDERGRADUATE STUDY
*"Licenciaturas"*

Applications are made through the official Portuguese website for higher education, the *"Direção Geral do Ensino Superior"* (DGES). The closing date for standard applications is in February of the year of entry. You should have your high school diploma or transcript, proof of your proficiency (Level B1 or B2) in Portuguese, and be ready to take an entrance exam, if applicable. The average yearly cost for a Bachelor's and a Master's Degree in most public universities in Portugal is between €1,000 - €3,500.

## MASTER'S
*"Mestrados"*

To get a master's degree, you must have a Bachelor's Degree, an equivalent diploma, or a transcript of your academic records. You can apply online directly to the university you are interested in. Contact the school's international office if they have one or the program department for more details on entry requirements. Be ready to show your portfolio if you are into arts, design, or fashion.

If the program you are interested in is taught in Portuguese, they might require a resume, a Curriculum Vitae (CV), and proof of Portuguese Language Proficiency of B1 or B2 level.

## PH.D. PROGRAM
*"Programas De Doutoramento"*

You must have a master's degree to enroll in a Ph.D. program. Get in touch with the university of your choice for more details and apply directly via their website.

## SOME POPULAR UNIVERSITIES IN PORTUGAL
*"Algumas Universidades Populares Em Portugal"*

- "Universidade de Porto"
- "Universiadade de Aveiro"
- "Universidade de Coimbra"
- "Universidade de Lisboa"
- "Universidade NOVA de Lisboa"
- "Universidade de Algarve"
- "Universidade de Beira Interior"
- "Universidade Católica Portuguesa"
- "Universidade de Lisbon ISCTE"
- "Universidade de Minho"

## "PROS" OF STUDYING IN PORTUGAL
*"Vantagens De Estudiar Em Portugal"*

- Low cost of tuition
- Top universities. Portuguese higher education is on par with European standards.
- Affordable costs of living.
- Safe country
- Amazing nightlife

- A beautiful country with lots of interest

- Students with families can have their spouses and children join them if they have a valid Portuguese Student Permit.

## "CONS" OF STUDYING IN PORTUGAL
*"Desvantagens De Estudiar Em Portugal"*

- Some universities will have amenities that are inferior to other European universities.

- English is widely spoken, but most undergraduate courses are taught in Portuguese, so you will be better off if you speak the language.

- If you can't afford the $1,000-$3,000 yearly college fees and must work, you will get paid the minimum wage, probably struggle financially, and might end up with a less expensive degree.

*Cork Backpack, Portugal*

# 17

## BUREAUCRACY IN PORTUGAL

### "BUROCRACIA EM PORTUGAL"

Bureaucracy is part of Portugal's everyday life, and soon it will be part of yours if you plan to settle in the country. Foreigners complain a lot about paperwork in Portugal, whether it is the long waiting time or the fact that they will send you from one service to the other to get the correct document. The good part is that most of it can be done online, like paying your phone bills or rent or bank transactions.

### FISCAL IDENTIFICATION NUMBER
### *"NÚMERO DE IDENTIFICAÇÃO FISCAL" - NIF*

If you plan on living in Portugal, the ideal is to arrive with a NIF, the Portuguese Tax Number, or *"Número de Identificação Fiscal."* NIF is a unique nine-digit number issued to each person. It will appear on your tax and Portuguese citizenship identity cards and is needed to deal with all kinds of transactions in the country, from getting your phone subscription, buying property, renting property long-term, signing up for utilities, and getting your residency permit, to paying your taxes, enrolling at a school, opening bank accounts, and so on.

Most applicants let their lawyer get it on their behalf or apply for it online through *"nifonline. pt"*. Usually, the embassy where you apply for your visa will obtain it for you because you don't have to be a resident of Portugal to get one. But suppose you don't have one before traveling. In that case, you can easily apply for it at the Tax Office in Portugal (*Finanças - Direcção-Geraldos Impostos*), or the *"Loja do Cidadão"* (Citizen Bureau) in person or by mail. You can even have a friend get it for you.

When issued for business purposes, it's called *"Número de Identificação de Pessoa Coletiva"* or Collective Person ID Number (NIPC). Obtaining a NIF is easy and quick unless you face long lines or delays in which case it can be a headache.

> **Note**: Having a NIF does not automatically make you a Tax Resident in Portugal.

## WHAT YOU NEED TO GET YOUR NIF
*"De Que Precisa Para Pedir O Nif"*

- Valid passport/ID card
- Proof of residence (outside of Portugal if you are a non-resident, residence permit if you are a resident in Portugal).
- Birth certificates for children with no passport.

> **Note**: A NIF never expires; hence doesn't need to be renewed.

## THE CITIZEN BUREAU
*"A Casa Do Cidadâo"*

The *"Casa do Cidadão"* or *"Loja de Cidadão"* is like a "multipurpose administrative service center" that houses different administrative branches, either SEF, Tax, Passport, Social Security Services, Driver's License, etc.

If you can, go early in the morning, and avoid going there during summer break, because that's when the Portuguese nationals who live abroad return home. They usually need to renew or get their documents done because it is easier and less expensive in Portugal than at a Portuguese consulate or embassy.

So, try to time your visit if you want to avoid waiting in line, which can still happen even if you have an appointment. And make sure you are getting the right ticket from the ticket dispenser if you don't want to be sent back in line.

## PORTUGAL IMMIGRATION AND BORDER SERVICE
*"SERVICO DE ESTRANGEIROS E FRONTEIRAS" - SEF*

After getting your travel visa, you will have four months to enter Portugal and book an appointment with your local *"Serviço De Estrangeiros E Fronteiras Direção Regional"* (SEF Regional Service Bureau) to get your biometrics done in order to get your residence permit.

The SEF Customer Service Bureau has a pre-booking system that allows you to book, cancel or reschedule your appointment by phone or online. Once you have made the appointment, you will receive an email confirmation. As a reminder, you will also get a text alert on your phone the day before your appointment.

If your appointment is several months away, keep the email or confirmation letter as proof. You will visit SEF each time you need to renew your residency until you reach the 5-year mark when you can apply for permanent residence.

## WHO SHOULD VISIT SEF
*"Quem Precisa De Visitar O Sef"*

- Non-EU applicants for a residence permit
- EU citizens applying for a Residence Certificate (CRUE) *"Certificado do Registo de Cidadão da União Europeia"*
- Visa-Free Entry holders who need to extend their stay
- Short-Stay Schengen visa holders who need to extend their stay
- Temporary-Stay visa/residence visa holders who need to extend their stay

## WHAT YOU WILL NEED FOR SEF
*"De Que Irá Precisar De Visitar O Sef"*

Before visiting SEF, try to find out which documents you need to bring. Here is a general list:

- Valid Passport or Other Valid Travel Documents
- 2 Recent Passport Pictures
- Valid Residence Visa
- Permission for SEF to Request Criminal Records
- Proof of Accommodation

- Proof of Financial Support or Sufficient Funds
- Work Contracts, if applicable
- A Declaration proving the Absence of Debts issued by the Inland Revenue and Customs Authority and by Social Security, if applicable

## PORTUGAL NATIONAL HEALTH SERVICES– SNS
## *"SERVICO NACIONAL DE SAÚDE"*

You'll need a unique identifying number (*Utente*) to access public healthcare in Portugal. Once you officially get your residence permit, you can apply for your SNS number. For EU citizens, you can register with your *"Certificado do Registo de Cidadão da União Europeia"* (CRUE), also known as the Residency Certificate.

You should register at your local health center (*Centro de Saúde*); it is important that you go to the one nearest your home address. There might be some waiting time; this is Portugal, after all. Look for the ticket dispenser, get one, and have something to do to help you pass the time. If you don't speak Portuguese, Google Translate might be helpful, or any other translation app. And once done, you will be free to schedule a doctor's appointment.

## WHAT YOU WILL NEED FOR YOUR *"UTENTE"*
*"De Que Irá Precisar Para Solicitar O Seu Número De Utente"*

- Valid Passport
- Proof of Residency (Residence Permit)
- NIF

- Social Security Number (only if you're employed in Portugal)
- Portuguese Phone Number

## RESIDENCE PERMIT
*"Cartão De Residência"*

The first five years of your residency in Portugal are classified as Temporary Residency. You get a Permanent Residence Permit after you have lived and/or worked in the country for five years, which means you will renew your residency permit several times over five years.

## WHAT YOU WILL NEED FOR YOUR RESIDENCE PERMIT
*"De Que Irá Precisar Para Solicitar O Seu Cartão De Residência"*

- Passport with Visa or any other Valid Traveling Document
- Proof of Legal Entry and Duration of Stay in Portugal
- Proof of Health Insurance
- A Signed Application giving SEF access to your Portuguese Criminal Record
- Criminal Record Certificate from any country where you have resided for over a year, which can be your country of origin
- A Declaration proving the Absence of Debts issued by the Inland Revenue and Customs Authority and by Social Security

*Braganza, Portugal*

## TAXES IN PORTUGAL
*"Impostos Em Portugal"*

You will not face any tax responsibility unless you become a tax resident in Portugal. To become a tax resident, you must spend more than 183 days of the year in the country, in which case you may have to pay tax on your worldwide income unless you are eligible for special tax status through Portugal's NHR (Non-Habitual Resident) Tax System.

You will fall under the NHR tax regime if you have a Golden Visa, a D7 Visa, and a D2 Visa. The NHR will allow you to transfer your tax residency to Portugal. You will then either pay only 20% of the taxes or be excluded from the tax payment requirements.

However, you will pay the same income tax as ordinary residents for other types of local income. Your pension income will then be taxed at a flat rate of 10%, including Retirement Savings and Life Insurance.

Foreign Interest, Dividends, Rent, and Property Capital Gains can be exempted from taxation. You can't have been taxed in Portugal five years before your application to be eligible. This doesn't apply to Corporate Tax.

It would be best if you referred to a professional tax advisor to know more because each case is different. Also, as a Golden Visa holder, you can maintain your immigration status whether you're a Portugal tax resident or not.

In 2019, the Portuguese Tax & Customs Authority (PTA) officially announced that buying or selling cryptocurrency in Portugal is tax-free. This is because crypto is viewed as a form of payment rather than an asset. In a word, Portugal won't tax you on cryptocurrency gains, but only if they are not the source of your professional or business activities.

When buying property anywhere in Portugal, you must pay several taxes, and Portugal taxes real estate quite heavily. There are three taxes for property: the Municipal Property Tax (IMI), the Municipal Real Estate Transfer Tax (IMT), and Stamp Duty (IS). (See the chapter about Property Taxes under Portugal Golden Visa). There's also a tax on the rent that the landlord should pay, so get that sorted out before signing.

> **Note**: You will not pay an Inheritance or Wealth Tax in Portugal.

## BANKING IN PORTUGAL
*"Serviço Bancário Em Portugal"*

Before you leave for Portugal, review all your bank accounts, and notify the banks of your relocation. Consider online international banking, which makes transferring and managing funds between countries easier.

You can open a bank account in Portugal even if you are a foreigner, an ex-pat, or a non-resident. You can even open an account in Portugal from anywhere in the world because Portugal does not apply any restrictions on the eligibility of banking clients. Banks generally open between 8:30 am – 3:00 pm, with a few open on Saturday mornings.

## MONEY
*"Dinheiro"*

Like the rest of the European Union, Portugal uses the Euro as its currency. It comes in 5, 10, 20, 50, 100, 200, and 500-euro bills, 1, 2, 5, 10, 20, and 50 cents, and €1, €2 coins. Check the Exchange Rate before traveling or buying property, even though the dollar and the euro are almost equal.

Visa, Mastercard, and American Express debit or credit cards are accepted in Portugal, even though there will be cases where you will need cash because cash is widely used in Portugal.

You can bring as much cash as you want to Portugal, but you should declare any amount that is over 10,000 euros at Customs. The other option is to wait to be in Portugal and withdraw cash from the many ATMs available.

> **Note**: The slang word for Money in Portuguese is *"Grana.* Remember to replace the comma with a period

when writing big numbers in Portugal. For example, €10,000 will be written as € 10.000 in Portugal.

## WHAT YOU NEED TO OPEN A BANK ACCOUNT IN PORTUGAL

*"O Que Precisa Para Abrir Uma Conta Bancária Em Portugal"*

- Proof of Identification (Passport, Residence Permit, ID Card, Driver's License)

- Proof of Address (a recent utility bill or lease contract)

- Portuguese NIF Number

- Proof of income/Employment (Work Contract, Pay Stubs, etc.)

- Portuguese Phone Number

- Cash Deposit for new accounts

## SOME OF THE COMMON BANKING SERVICES IN PORTUGAL

*"Alguns Serviços Bancários Comuns Em Portugal"*

There are over 150 local and foreign banks to pick from, including international ones. You can also send money anywhere in the world for lesser fees and at a mid-market exchange rate when you open a Wise multi-currency account or similar banking systems. Also, some banks have no maintenance or debit card fees and standard transactions such as ATM withdrawals. And you can transfer euros for free or negligible fees within the Eurozone. Here is a list of the type of banking services accompanied by a few bank names.

148

- Checking accounts (Caixa Geral de Depósitos, Millennium BCP, Novo Banco, Banco BPI, Banco Santander Totta)
- Loans and Overdrafts
- Mortgages
- Savings and Investments (Banco Carregosa, BiG (Banco de Investimento Global), Banco Finantia, Banco Invest)
- Insurance
- Digital and Online Banking
- Mobile Banking (ActivoBank, Banco N26, Caixa Geral de Depósitos, Millennium BCP, Novo Banco)
- Business Banking
- Expat Services
- Trading Services

## TYPES OF BANKS IN PORTUGAL
*"Tipos De Bancos Em Portugal"*

- Private National Banks
- International Banks (Abanca, Barclays, BBVA, BNP Paribas, Citibank, Credit Agricole, Deutsche Bank, ING Bank)
- Public Retail Banks
- Regional Cooperative Banks
- Investment Banks
- Savings Banks

*Flores Island, Azores, Portugal*

# 18

## HEALTHCARE IN PORTUGAL

"SAÚDE EM PORTUGAL"

**PORTUGAL BASIC HEALTHCARE**
*"Assistência Médica Básica Em Portugal"*

You can get basic health insurance in Portugal through employment, the European Health Insurance Card (EHIC) if you are from the EU/EEA or Switzerland, or private health insurance if you are a non-EU national. After getting your Residence Card, you will register with your local Health Care Center or *"Centros de Saude."* You will then receive your Healthcare Card or *"Cartao de Utente,"* which you will show every time you need to access Portuguese healthcare services.

## WHAT YOU NEED TO REGISTER FOR HEALTH INSURANCE
*"De Que Precisa Para Fazer O Seguro De Saúde"*

- Your Social Security Card
- Your Passport or National ID card
- Your Residence Permit

As a resident, you will get an SNS (National Health Service) number and be assigned a family doctor. You will be able to use their website to make appointments. Their services are free for children under 18 and those over 65 and give you access to emergency treatments and psychiatric and maternity care, but not dental care.

Contraception is widely available in Portugal; you won't need a prescription for birth control pills, and condoms are sold in any supermarket or drugstore. Abortion is legal in Portugal in the first ten weeks of pregnancy, and the insurance usually covers the costs. You will first consult your General Practitioner (GP) or Family Doctor and be given three days of reflection before the procedure.

If you use the Public Health System, seeing a doctor can cost as little as €5.00 and will be free if you are unemployed, a chronic patient, under 18, pregnant, or have a low salary. Even if most services are free, visiting emergency rooms or diagnosing exams might require payment.

Most health centers in Portugal are open from 8 am to 8 pm. However, the health centers' quality of services will depend on where you live. That is why most people have both Public and Private Coverage. It will be up to you to schedule your medical tests at a lab/clinic within the network. Always ask the doctors beforehand if the labs or clinics are in the SNS network and if the tests are covered. Do not hesitate to ask questions if you need more clarification.

Portugal's Social Health Coverage Program has yet to go online. Though there are electronic patient files at clinics and hospitals, there have yet to be any electronic medical records.

> **Note**: The quality of care might be high, but your chances of seeing a specialist at a reasonable time might be low, so having both public and private healthcare might be a good choice.

## PRIVATE HEALTHCARE
*"Sistema De Saúde Privado"*

Expats living legally in Portugal can benefit from free basic healthcare, even though it is common for them to go for Private Health Insurance instead. If you are a non-resident or a temporary visitor to Portugal, you will need to purchase private health insurance to cover your stay, which is available at reasonable costs. For instance, you will pay 5% of the price in the US for insurance, and an appointment with a private doctor will cost around 40–50 euros. Private doctors also have shorter waiting lists and will mostly have English-speaking staff. Private coverage prices will range from €300 to €1,000 a year, depending on the insurance company, your health, and your age. Some of Portugal's Largest Private Health Insurance Companies are Allianz Care, Cigna, Globalityn, Medis, and Multicare.

## PHARMACIES
*"Farmácias"*

Pharmacies' general opening hours are 9 am-7 pm on weekdays (with a lunch break between 1-3 pm) and 9 am-1 pm on Saturdays. *"Farmácias de Serviço"* are duty pharmacies open past 8 pm for emergencies. The SNS website provides a list of all pharmacies. You will find out that medical costs are graded as follow: 90% – Grade A, 69% – Grade B, 37% – Grade C, and 15% – Grade D.

## RECOMMENDED HOSPITALS
*"Hospitais Recomendados"*

- "Hospital da Luz Torres de Lisboa" (former British Hospital in Lisbon)
- "CMIL Cliica Medica Internacional de Lisboa (Lisbon)"
- "CUF Cascais"
- "Hospital Cruz Vermelha (Lisbon)"
- "Centro Hospitalar Lisboa Norte (Lisbon)"
- "Luzdoc Servica Medico Internacional (Lagos)"
- "Hospital Partiuclar do Algarve (Portima)"
- "Hospital São Goncalo de Lagos"

## MENTAL HEALTHCARE
*"Sistema De Saúde Mental"*

Unfortunately, Portugal has higher than the EU average levels of depression and substance abuse. Despite this, Portugal's mental healthcare service is not as developed as in several other countries.

Consult your General Practitioner or Family Doctor first if you need access to mental health services through the SNS. Depending on your situation and where you live, your doctor can prescribe medication or refer you for counseling to a specialist, a psychiatric unit, or an emergency unit.

Private insurance can give you access to a wide range of specialties without a referral from your General Practitioner.

Mental health care services in Portugal are provided through:

- Local services
- Regional services
- Psychiatric hospitals

**Note**: The police will arrest and take anyone showing erratic behavior to a mental facility.

## MENTAL HEALTHCARE FOR CHILDREN
*"Saúde Mental Para Crianças"*

The Pediatric Hospitals in Lisbon, Porto, and Coimbra have mental health centers for children and teenagers (in Portuguese).

**Europe's Medical Emergency Number is 112, free of charge, 24/7.**

Here are the main emergency support lines, available 24/7

- For illness: *"Linha Saúde 23"*; 808 24 24 24, available 24/7
- In case of missing children: *"Linha Criança Desaparecida"*, call 116 000.
- Children helpline: *"SOS Criança"* 116 111

155

## ALTERNATIVE THERAPIES
*"Terapias Alternativas"*

76% of patients have used alternative therapy in Lisbon. This includes acupuncture, chiropractic, osteopathy, naturopathy, herbal medicine, and massage. You must pay out of pocket unless a private insurance policy covers it.

## SOME USEFUL MEDICAL EXPRESSIONS
*"Algunas Expressões Médical Úteis"*

- *"Centro de Saúde"* = Health Centre
- *"Hospital"* = Hospital
- *"Medicina"* = Medicine
- *"Emergência"* = Emergency
- *"Maternidade"* = Maternity
- *"Chame uma ambulância"* = Call an ambulance!
- *"Gostaria de ver/consular um medico"* = I would like to see a doctor.
- *"Gostaria de marcar uma consulta"* = I'd like to make an appointment.

*Umbrella Street, Agueda, Portugal*

# 19

## LIFE IN PORTUGAL

### "VIDA EM PORTUGAL"

### WEATHER
*"Tempo"*

Where you live in Portugal will play a huge role in how you perceive the country. The climate in Portugal is good for most of the year. Summers are generally hot, and the houses lose heat in the summer (or don't let it in or a mixture of the two).

Traditional homes are relatively comfortable in summer, even without air conditioning. A simple piece of advice is to close your windows and keep down the shutters during the day (or between 10 AM and 4 PM) to avoid your house heating up too much.

However, you will get cold gray winters from December to February. Am I insinuating that it gets cold in Portugal? What happened to the 365 days of sunshine? It will always be warmer than in some northern countries because temperatures rarely go below zero.

Unfortunately, most houses don't have central heating, so sweaters, blankets, and portable heaters will be your companions during cold nights. If you are sensitive to cold, wintertime in an old house in the countryside - while idyllic in summer - can be unpleasant with no thermal insulation and no central heating, so keep that in mind while buying or renting an old house.

## COST OF LIVING
*"Custo De Vida"*

Portugal is getting a little more expensive every day but is still cheaper than most Western European countries. Housing and other utilities are more expensive in the main cities, suburbs, and surrounding cities. The cost of living in Portugal for most people is between $1,000 and $1,500/month, depending on where you live. You'll barely be able to get by in a city like Porto with minimum wage unless you get a roommate, live in a modest apartment, or outside Porto and Lisbon.

Southern Portugal, on average, is 20% more expensive than the north. For example, Porto is about 15% more costly than Viana do Castelo, which lies further north. Despite the general increase in living costs, prices for things like movies, museums, and even traveling inside the country are still reasonable.

If you're a student and want to be close to the university, renting a room will cost around 200–250€/month. But if you buy a one-room apartment at the current interest rate, you can pay as little as 250€/month mortgage, especially if you buy an old one and renovate.

With prices going up, it is hard to say how much you will spend per month. Utilities (Electricity + water + telephone + internet) bills will be around €100/month per person, while groceries might average around €150/month/per person. Transportation (3-zone bus and metro pass) is around 40€; if you own a car, expect to pay an average of 150€/month. These prices are only here to show you how much you might spend because it will all depend on your location and lifestyle.

But remember that in Portugal, employees get paid 14 salaries per year, which gives people more margin for extra spending, and ex-pats tend to earn twice as much as the average Portuguese.

## CONSUMER GOODS
*"Bens De Consume"*

Cosmetics and toiletries can be expensive in Portugal as some processed food, such as breakfast cereals. Meat and cheese are more expensive but of better quality compared to places like the UK and are way worth the money.

Cars in Portugal are expensive due to the tax regime, and rents are high relative to the earning power of the average Portuguese. But for foreigners with overseas income, this is fine, which explains why Portugal remains affordable for most ex-pats.

The country has many chain stores like Pingo Doce, Continente, Mini-Preço, or French chain stores, such as Intermarché, Auchan, and Leclerc, where you can go grocery shopping.

## UTILITIES
*"Serviços De Utilidade Pública"*

If you are renting, the utilities will be already installed. If they are included in the rental contract, the landlord or the agent will itemize the amounts at the end of the year.

Otherwise, utilities can take up to 5 days to install, and you may need to pay for some services upfront, like gas line inspections. The energy costs in Portugal are high; they will spike during hot summers or cold winters.

Internet & cable can take 2 to 3 weeks to install, sometimes less, depending on the region and the service provider you use. You can get your landline, internet, and TV services from the same provider. If taking over the utilities from a previous owner or tenant, make sure that the person has canceled their contract. If not, making a transfer (*Transferência*) of accounts will be necessary, which is generally easier than setting up a new account.

You will likely use the *"Multibanco"* system to pay for your utilities. You will need a Portuguese bank account and your NIF to set up the account.

**Note**: All cancellations must be made online or by mail.

*Benagil Cave, Algarve, Portugal*

## ELECTRICITY
*"Eletricidade"*

*"Entidade Reguladora dos Serviços Energéticas"* is an independent energy regulator or watchdog that will arbitrate disputes between you and the energy supplier. Try to review the meter readings with the previous owners/renters to verify that there are no extra charges since the latest bills.

Some suppliers allow customers to enter their monthly meter readings and only pay for the energy used. At the same time, some apartments come with a Remote Electronic Counter, which enables remote reading, meaning you can get disconnected remotely when an overdue bill remains unpaid.

The electricity supply may be cut during peak electricity usage periods or storms. This happens very often in many regions. Consider installing a generator or a UPS system for computers.

163

The standard electricity supply in Portugal is around 220 volts (V) AC, with a frequency of 50 hertz (HZ). Some old houses still have the 110-volt supply, although this is rare now. A Power Surge Protector is also recommended to protect appliances (computers, TVs, fax machines) when the power supply resumes.

The most used provider in Portugal is EDP *(Energias de Portugal)*, but it's not the only one. Also, Portugal uses the standard European two-pin plug and socket. If you need one, adapters are available at most supermarkets, airports, hotels, and shops.

## WHAT YOU WILL NEED TO SET UP AN ELECTRICITY BILL
*"O Que Vai Precisar Para Pedir A Ligaçao De Electridade"*

- Passport, Identity Card, or Residency Permit
- Your name, address, and the name of the previous occupier/tenant (if applicable)
- Tax Number of the account holder if it is set up by a private individual or IVA card (*Numero Fiscal de Contribuinte de Empresas*) if it is a business
- The power required (from 1.15 Kw to 41 Kw)
- The current reading of the meter (*Leitura do Contador*)
- Bank details if you want to make monthly payments
- Address to which the bills should be sent
- And the address to which the contract should be sent

## GAS
*"Gás"*

Portugal has no coal mines, oil wells, or gas fields. All of its natural gas is imported from mainly North and West Africa. Gas is widely used for heating during winter, water heating, and cooking in Portugal.

The 2022 global energy crisis, a result of the COVID-19 pandemic, has left much of the world facing shortages and increased prices in oil, gas, and electricity, and Portugal was no exception. To tackle the problem, Portugal has taken a few actions, such as turning off indoor decorative lighting earlier than usual and slightly lowering central heating temperatures because it's in the winter period that the gas supply troubles intensify across Europe.

There are three types of Gas in Portugal.

Mains Gas is used for appliances and heating, and *"Galp Energia"* must approve all installations. As the new tenant or property owner, choose and contact your local supplier and agree on a payment plan. Make an appointment with a Gas Technician (*Técnico Credenciado do Gás*) to have the meter read, and the gas turned on.

Bottled Gas (*Botijas de Gás*) is mostly butane gas (although propane is available). It can be bought in small quantities (usually 10, 15, or 20 kilograms) and is generally kept in the kitchen under the sink. Bottled gas is often used for gas-type heaters during winter in houses without central heating. It may also heat water.

Gas Tanks (*Contentor de Gás*) usually contain 1,000 liters of liquid gas. It is more common in rural areas and is stored outside the house. Let your insurance company know if you are using a gas tank (charges may be slightly higher).

> **Note:** Call the supplier immediately to report a Gas Leak *(Fuga de Gás)*. The ERSE "*Entidade Reguladora dos Serviços* Energéticos" or Portuguese Energy Services Regulatory Authority, has a list of gas suppliers you can call.

## WHAT YOU WILL NEED TO OPEN A GAS ACCOUNT
*"De Que Vai Precisar Para Ter Gás Em Casa"*

- Registration Number of the Meter
- Name of previous tenant/owner, if possible
- Name and account details of new tenant/owner
- Passport or Identity Card
- Residency Card or Proof of Residency

## WATER
*"Água"*

First, it's safe to drink tap water in Portugal since it conforms to EU standards. However, suppose you feel concerned about the water quality or don't like the taste, especially in rural areas. If that is the case, you should buy a filter, a cheaper and more environmentally friendly alternative to bottled water.

When hit by severe or extreme drought, which many of the country's southern parts regularly suffer, Portugal will likely temporarily restrict water use for activities like gardening or car washing to maintain water supplies.

Water installation is faster, usually two days, but it can be the hardest because it is generally paid separately to each municipality; each has its provider and sets its prices. Contact your local town hall to find information about your local supplier, and once you do, call them to set up your water. You will pay your water bills bi-monthly.

Your water payments will likely be included in your monthly rent if you move to an apartment complex. Still, in some rural areas, sometimes having the main water connection is impossible, meaning you would rely on a water tank which can be expensive. Keep that in mind before buying property.

## WHAT YOU WILL NEED TO OPEN A WATER ACCOUNT
*"De Que Vai Precisar Para Pedir A Ligação De Água"*

- Copy of your ID (Passport or ID card)
- Portuguese Tax Number (NIF)
- The Last Meter Readings
- Bank Details if you want to make direct payments

*Ericeira, Portugal*

## GREEN ENERGY
*"Energia Verde"*

Portugal has invested a lot in its renewable energy production. Lisbon was awarded the title of European Green Capital for 2020. So, if you are looking for green energy options, sign up for Green Utilities in Portugal. Despite the constant sunshine, wind and hydropower generate the most energy, even if the country still gets most of its power from fossil fuels. Search online to see if one of the 100% green energy providers is in your area.

## HEATING
*"Aquecimento"*

Depending on where you choose to live, you might end up with rainy and cold winters. Those winters might be even more brutal once you discover that the charming old house you are renting is not insulated. Add to that the electricity bills, and you will understand why the energy costs are so high in Portugal. So, remember that a modern home might not have all the charms of an old house, but the chances for it to have insulation will be much higher.

Fortunately, there are many options for heating your home in Portugal. Gas, solar panels, or electricity can all be used for central heating and hot water. Some places have fireplaces. Some others will have pellet stoves, which are prone to making noise and needing more maintenance than traditional fireplaces. You can also install a hydraulic underfloor heating/cooling system that uses water for heating & cooling and can be found in modern homes, which is much more efficient than radiators or heaters.

## VIRTUAL PRIVATE NETWORK (VPN)
*"Redes Privadas Virtuais"*

If you're in Portugal and want to unblock region-locked content or enjoy improved online privacy on public Wi-Fi networks, you'll need a VPN. Once you have one, connect to a server in Portugal to get a Portuguese IP address.

ExpressVPN and NordVPN are among the best VPNs in Portugal. ExpressVPN has the best speeds and security features for Portugal, so it's the top VPN choice for now.

## TELEVISION
*"Televisão"*

There's a wide range of English-language TV available, so culturally, you won't have to watch Portuguese TV at all if you choose not to. And this, rather than Portuguese itself, is one of the most significant barriers to foreigners living in Portugal because nothing will force you to speak Portuguese.

## MAIL
*"Correio"*

Before you leave, cancel all subscriptions and complete the appropriate forms at your post office to ensure your mail is forwarded to your new address in Portugal.

If you are already in Portugal, go to your local Post Office to fill out the appropriate forms and directly contact any institution (banks, insurance companies, cable, etc.) you might get mail from and give them your new address. Otherwise, try services like traveling mailboxes; they will scan the outside of your envelopes and forward your mail and packages anywhere in the world.

## PRESCRIPTION DRUGS
*"Medicamentos De Prescrição"*

If you or a family member takes prescription drugs, purchase additional quantities to last you a couple of months. Do your research and try to find out if you can get the same prescription in Portugal or the equivalent. Contact your doctor and get a copy of the medical file related to the condition. Once you are settled in Portugal, find a doctor through your insurance health company.

*Nazaré, Portugal*

# 20

## GETTING AROUND PORTUGAL

### "DESLOCAR-SE EM PORTUGAL"

#### DRIVER'S LICENCE
*"Carta De Condução"*

Amerian and Canadian driving licenses will soon be valid in Portugal, which means drivers can use the document issued by their country of origin until the end of its validity. At this point, they will switch to a Portuguese license. You can only drive in Portugal with your country-issued driver's license for a period that should be at most 185 days if you are not a legal resident yet. Once you get your residence permit, you will need to exchange your driver's license for a Portuguese one unless you are moving to Portugal from another EU country, in which case you won't need to do the exchange.

Exchanging your foreign driver's license for a Portuguese driver's license will vary depending on your country of origin and period of residence. So, check with your country of origin to know if they have any bilateral agreements with Portugal for driving.

## BUYING A CAR
*"Comprar Um Carro"*

Buying a car in Portugal is expensive. It is even more expensive when it is an imported car. However, when buying from a dealership (*Concessionário*), they will take care of all the paperwork. Some even sell car insurance.

Now, imagine you find someone willing to sell you their car. Make sure the seller is the valid owner of the vehicle. You will need to confirm that the documentation provided by the seller matches the vehicle's identification numbers. You may also inherit any fines or outstanding debt attached to the car. Before closing the deal, you should always check with a notary (*Notário*) at the Civil Registry Office (*Conservatoria do Registo Civil*).

> **Note**: You don't need a visa or be a resident to buy a car in Portugal if you can show the following:

- Proof of Address (a recent utility bill, lease contract or rental agreement, proof of purchase of real estate)
- Your NIF
- Your ID (passport, driving license, residence permit)

## TRANSPORTATION
*"Transporte"*

If you live in a big city like Porto or Lisbon, you will take public transportation, hence the importance of learning conversational Portuguese to get around.

Trains are good along the western coast between Lisbon and Porto. They are Ok in the south and average everywhere else.

The Expresso Bus Network is excellent and cheap, and you can buy the Pass online. It covers most places in the country, is comfortable and the buses are frequent. Secondary bus networks are good too, but you usually must book and purchase tickets at their departure locations.

Having a car in smaller towns is essential. You may take the train or bus into the big cities, but a car is much easier to get from one small town to another. You might need to rent one before getting your own. Some rental car agencies like Europcar or Guerin have branches throughout Portugal.

What about bikes? Well, with the half-exception of the Alentejo plains in the South, Portugal is a hilly country. It is not only hard going uphill, but there are few bike lanes unless you live in a big city like Porto.

The country has four and six-lane toll motorways and good secondary roads, all in excellent condition, mostly due to the road tolls.

*Funchal, Madeira Island, Portugal*

# 21

## REAL ESTATE IN PORTUGAL

"MERCADO IMOBILIÁRIO EM PORTUGAL"

**BUYING PROPERTY IN PORTUGAL**
*"Comprar Imóveis Em Portugal"*

Before purchasing land in Portugal, it is essential to make sure that you can build on it. You will also want to know what you can or can't do with it. So, go to the *"Câmara Municipal"* and ask for the PDM or *"Regulamento do Plano Director Municipal"* (the Council Plan), which is specific for each council. It will give you information about land specifications and building regulations. If you revive an old business, say a café or a restaurant, check if the place is up to the current code and standard, if the commercial license hasn't expired, and if it can be renewed.

If you are thinking of investing in an estate in Portugal, first check out the properties around the area you want to buy in. Have they been selling lately? Is there any important immigration community? If the answer is no, investing in that area will likely not be a good idea because it will be harder to re-sell.

177

> **Note:** If you are looking into buying property in Portugal and are unsure where to start, check out BuyProperty.com. Not only will they help you find the best property, but they will also show you through analytics if a property is over or undervalued and how much you can expect to earn if you are looking into investing.

The amount you spend acquiring real estate in Portugal will depend on your finances, needs, and wants. A new house in the city will cost at least €600,000. But, if that house is in a low-density area, your costs go down to €400,000. And if you buy an old house instead, you can renovate it for at least €350,000. You won't pay any property tax as long as you don't rent it. If you do, expect a 28% flat rate real estate income tax.

The materials for building or renovating have become more expensive, making it challenging to stick to a budget or deadlines. Foreigners in Portugal stay in the big cities because it is more convenient to travel, and they can get better and faster access to hospitals and the art scene (theatres, galleries, etc.) Also, in case they must return to their home country, it is easier to sell an apartment in a major city than a big house in a small village.

Since January 2022, you can't purchase real estate in Lisbon (which includes Sintra, Cascais, the Algarve, etc.), Porto, and the coastal towns to obtain a Portugal Golden Visa. Only properties in low-density areas, such as the Azores, and the inland territories, are now eligible for the Portuguese Golden Visa. Also, keep in mind that other areas like Braga can be great investments.

> **Note**: You can purchase real estate with Bitcoin and other cryptocurrencies through intermediaries and qualify for a golden visa.

The €500,000 investment golden visa threshold allows you to choose any property anywhere in Madeira: which can go from a brand-new development in the center of Funchal, the capital, to an old traditional "Quinta" in a banana plantation or an apartment at the beach.

You can invest in a 30-year-old property for rehabilitation or renovation. The restoration of an old property can go from light rehabilitation (minor repairs typically in the bathroom and kitchen) to exceptional, with the new building being of a much higher standard than the old ones. Be attentive and considerate of the context and cultural value of the surroundings during the rehabilitation process.

If you invest in a low-density area, there is a 20% discount available on Golden Visa property investment thresholds. Also, with a Golden Visa, you can maintain residency rights without ever becoming a tax resident. However, when buying property anywhere in Portugal, you must pay several taxes.

There are three taxes for property in Portugal: The Municipal Property Tax (IMI) must be paid every year starting from the moment you acquire the property. The Municipal Real Estate Transfer Tax (IMT) is imposed on the real estate transaction), and the Stamp Duty (IS) is imposed on the purchase and sale of a property.

## LANDLORDS
*"Senhorios"*

Whether you became a landlord through investment for the Golden Visa or have purchased a property in Portugal, if you turn your home into a rental, you must first get a permit and pass the safety requirements. For short-term rentals, this is if you turn your property into a vacation rental, you will pay a tourist tax. But for long-term rentals, you will need to register the lease and issue tax receipts. Hiring an agent to take care of everything might be helpful.

If you own an apartment in a building, you may have to pay maintenance fees to cover maintenance costs like painting, window treatments, elevator or pool repairs, etc.

If you need to make renovations and need the tenants out, you must give them at least two months' notice before putting a term to the contract. Before evicting a tenant, first, send them a notification. You can evict someone if they haven't paid their rent for three months, have caused damage to the property, if there is a breach of the contract, or if you want to live in it. If there is a dispute between you and your tenants and you are unsure what to do, contact a lawyer or go to Social Security to get some help.

*River Almondo, Santarém, Portugal*

**TENANTS/RENTERS**
*"Inquilinos/Arrendatários"*

**WHAT TO KNOW BEFORE RENTING IN PORTUGAL**

## *"O Que Saber Antes De Arrendar Em Portugal"*

- Only sign a contract after visiting the home or send someone reliable to look at it.

- Take pictures of everything before you move in (furniture, appliances, gas, electricity meters). Cover all your bases in case of a dispute.

- Make sure all repairs are done before you move in.

- Review the contract and check what is included and their policies about smoking and having pets.

- Ask where to find the fuse box, the heater, and the gas tank. Ask how to use them if you don't know.

- Set up the utilities as soon as you have signed your contract. Otherwise, you might end up spending a few days with no water or heat.

**RENTING AN APARTMENT IN PORTUGAL**

## *"Arrendar Um Apartamento Em Portugal"*

There are two types of rentals in Portugal, short-term and long-term leases. If you choose to live in a big city, you will probably rent an apartment unless you are a student and can have access to the student's housing. If you are looking for a house and still want to be in a big city, look in the suburbs/outskirts.

Some landlords would rather make short-term leases to tourists than rent long-term. Since it's challenging to find a long-term rental, you should start by renting short-term while you look for something long-term. Most rentals come furnished or partially furnished. T1 is a one-bedroom, and T2 is a two-bedroom apartment.

The cost of renting an apartment in Portugal will vary according to your budget and where you choose to live. People who live in big cities share rent costs since the rent is generally higher. Having a roommate or flatmate might be a good option if you are single. There are different ways to find housing; look online, use Facebook groups, word-to-mouth, or go through real estate agencies.

Once you find a place to live, some landlords or agencies will ask for two- or three months' rent, and others might ask for a Security Deposit (*Caução*) that will be returned to you when your lease ends, on the condition that you didn't cause any significant damage to the rental.

Renting an apartment will cost less anywhere else than in Lisbon or Porto. Most landlords will make you sign a contract, which will specify the lease terms. Check if the utilities are included so you know how much more you will need to pay. They will also give you an inventory of all the furniture if the place is furnished.

> **Note**: If not offered a contract, always ask for one since it will protect you in case of a dispute.

You will soon find out that it is much easier to rent in rural areas, but the chances of finding a landlord who speaks English will also be minimal. They also might be more willing to rent with no contract, yet you will still need to show the same documents listed below. With or without a contract, always ask if the utilities are included. If you rent through an agency, you won't pay any fees; the landlords usually pay them.

Your rental contract will automatically renew unless you move out or the landlord kicks you out. If you move out, you will need to give at least two months' written notice before, and you can't sublet or sublease unless your contract says so.

A standard contract should include the following:

- Name and Identification of all parties renting
- Property address
- Rent Cost and Limit Date for payment
- Contract Duration

**WHAT YOU NEED FOR THE LEASE**

## *"O Que Presica Para Um Contrato De Arrendamento"*

- Tax number NIF
- ID (Passport, Driver's License, Residence Permit)
- Bank Statement
- Tax returns
- Any Proof of Employment (work contract, paychecks, etc.)

*Douro Vineyard, Portugal*

# 22

## WHERE TO LIVE IN PORTUGAL

### "ONDE VIVER EM PORTUGAL"

Once you get your visa, you can live anywhere in Portugal, except if you have a Golden Visa, which has restrictions (see the chapter about Retiring in Portugal).

If you are still deciding where to live, rent furnished for a year and keep exploring before deciding until you find the place you will call home. The list below is not exhaustive; it is merely a glimpse of what Portugal has to offer.

Houses in the south are more colorful, which goes with the warmer weather, while houses in the north are mostly made of granite, giving them a more neutral tone. If the beach is not your top priority, you should live in the north. You will find a greener and hillier landscape, some cities will even have snow, and the beaches will be smaller but rockier.

## THE NORTH OF PORTUGAL
*"Norte De Portugal"*

### AVEIRO DISTRICT: THE VENICE OF PORTUGAL

## *"Zona De Aveiro: A Veneza De Portugal"*

Aveiro is in the center north of Portugal. It is a charming town famous for its canals, hence the Venice of Portugal nickname. The city is small enough to walk to the shopping malls and restaurants. It has a great university, which makes it the perfect place for ex-pats who want a smaller city with a lively downtown or a town suitable for families with young children. It has good public schools, is less rainy, and is less expensive than Porto.

You can shop at the Glicínias Plaza (which has everything, including a movie theater) and at the Fórum Aveiro, or you can attend their festival, Feira de Março. If you are a foodie, try the *"Farturas"* (they're like churros but thicker and bigger) and the *"Ovos Moles"* (a local pastry made of egg yolk and sugar.)

### THE AZORES

## *"Açores"*

Açores, pronounced Azores in English, are less developed than Madeira. They are in the Atlantic Ocean for over two hours by air from Lisbon. This nine-island archipelago is famous for its temperate climate, beaches, volcanic landscapes, and relaxing thermal baths. If you haven't visited yet, try to stay at least three to four weeks before moving there. The cost of living is considerably lower than in mainland

188

Portugal. Housing and food prices are generally lower, except for some imported products that are more expensive.

## BRAGA: THE RELIGIOUS CAPITAL

### *"Braga: Capital Religiosa"*

Braga is a top choice for foreigners who emigrate to Portugal. Here you will find the oldest Portuguese archdiocese, the Archdiocese of Braga of the Catholic Church, making Braga one of the oldest cities in Portugal. It is also famous for its Research Center on Nanotechnology and Medical Innovation.

However, the city has no beach, the summers are too hot, and it rains a lot during winter, causing floods and traffic all over the city. Besides that, the town is small enough to walk, but people don't walk that much. Although there's a public transit system, you will drive everywhere, school, work, and stores. It is hard to get around and be independent if you are in a wheelchair. But if you are a family with children, consider living on the outskirts, in places such as Briteiros or Vila Verde.

## BRAGANÇA DISTRICT

### *"Zona De Brangança"*

Bragança, pronounced Braganza in English, is in the northeast part of Portugal, about 255 km (158 miles) from Porto, 515 km (320 miles) from Lisbon, and 22 km (14 miles) from the Spanish border. There is no train service to Bragança. If you are coming from Lisbon, you can always take a train to Porto and catch a bus that will take over three hours to get to Bragança. It will take you five hours to drive from Lisbon to Bragança.

Like Porto, Bragança has a Mediterranean climate, with very wet winters and very hot summers, July being the hottest month and December the wettest. Winters are actually worse in Bragança as it is also one of the few cities in Portugal that experiences snow, January being the coldest month.

Depending on your health, walking around the city could be challenging because it's a hilly city, and since public transportation is limited, you will be better off getting a car. Unless you come here to retire, there are few job opportunities, and it lacks the nightlife you will find in big cities.

However, living in Bragança will take you back to medieval times, and the property prices for renting and buying are low.

## GUIMARÃES: THE BIRTHPLACE OF PORTUGAL

*"Guimarães: O Local De Nascimento De Portugal"*

UNESCO listed Guimarães as a World Heritage Site because this is where Afonso Henriques, the first king of Portugal, was born in 1109. It is 55km or 35 miles northeast of Porto and 1h15 away by train. It is a college town with "The University of Minho" that attracts Erasmus students from all over Europe.

Summers in Guimarães are short and dry, while winters can get chilly and cloudy. Although hilly, it is a walkable city with a reliable public system. Buses will take you to France and Spain, while the trains will take you to all the major cities.

There are two public hospitals, a private hospital, and several clinics. "Largo da Oliveira" is the central plaza and the city's heartbeat. At the same time, *"Feira de Velharias"* is a flea market

190

where the inhabitants sell anything they no longer want or need. These include toys, paintings, old magazines, rare books, jewelry, and clothing. Someone making $2000/month could have a nice life in Guimarães.

*Faro, Portugal*

## PORTO

### *"Oporto"*

Porto is the financial capital of Portugal and is famous for the Porto wine neither produced nor stored in Porto. Another thing Porto is renowned for is the *"Tripas à Moda do Porto,"* a dish made with beef tripe and intestines with lots of beans and cumin, which explains why people from Porto are called *"Tripeiros"* (tripe eaters). And let's not forget the football club that made Porto a name all around Europe: F.C. Porto.

Porto is a beautiful town with plenty of history, several universities, many start-ups, great food, and friendly, educated people. Some of its abandoned warehouses are being turned

191

into offices for software companies and start-ups. For some people, Porto emits *"Saudade,"* a reference to "a sense of loneliness and incompleteness." Not being as refined as Lisbon gives the city a feel of authenticity. Older women still wear homemade outfits in a rare shade of green you don't find anymore.

Porto has great airline connections and a modern and efficient metro system. It is a very walkable city and feels safe.

## WHY NOT PORTO
*"Porque Não Escolher Porto"*

Unfortunately, it is no longer eligible for Golden Visa Residential Real Estate Investment. One other downside to living in Porto is the weather. It has wetter and cooler winters than southern cities, so if you dream of finer weather, try Cascais.

## THE CENTER OF PORTUGAL
*"O Centro De Portugal"*

### COIMBRA: THE UNIVERSITY CITY
*"Coimbra: A Cidade Univertária"*

Coimbra is a beautiful town by the river Mondego and is part of the Portugal Silver Coast. It is a University City with one of the oldest universities in Europe. You can make a lot of profit if you buy property in Coimbra and rent it to the many students looking for accommodation. The city is right in the center of Portugal, making it the perfect place to travel from north to south. The accent is pretty standard, so if you want to learn Portuguese, try living there for a while.

## COVILHÃ.

Few people know this town. It's close to Serra Da Estrela, the highest peak in Portugal, which also happens to be a ski resort. It is just one hour's drive from the Spanish border, which can be convenient if you like a change of scenery from time to time. Covilhã is a small mountain city home to the Universidade da Beira Interior.

> **Note**: As a college town, it has many international students who come to study through the Erasmus program.

## LEIRIA

Leiria is the capital city of the Leiria District and has a mix of Mediterranean and Atlantic weather, with very cold winters and warm summers. It shares borders on the north with Coimbra. Although located a little further inland, the beautiful beaches of Portugal's Silver Coast are a short drive away. Being away from the coast means life in Leiria is affordable.

## NAZARÉ: NAH-ZAH-REH

Nazaré is an attractive coastal city for ex-pats and tourists alike. It is a little over an hour's drive from Lisbon, and people here love to fish and live a retired lifestyle. For people looking to move to Portugal's Silver Coast, Nazaré is an ideal destination because of its natural beauty, quality of life, simple and open-minded people, beaches, and reasonable cost of living. You can easily find a two-room apartment for around €500 per month.

## THE PORTUGAL SILVER COAST
*"O Costa Da Prata De Portugal"*

The Silver Coast is in the central region of Portugal, halfway between Porto and Lisbon. Like the rest of Portugal, it has a moderate climate. The area remains unexplored with its wilder and untouched coastline. It's far less developed than the south, less touristy, and a great alternative to the Algarve. It includes the historic cities of Tomar and Coimbra. It is a safe, inexpensive, and expat-friendly region with stunning beaches such as Peniche and Nazaré and is considered by some as "the best place to buy in the sun." Did we mention that this should be on your destination list if you were an avid surfer?

### VISEU

Viseu is in the countryside. It is a small, clean, beautiful city in the center of Portugal. Half an hour from the beach, surrounded by incredible mountains and hills, it has everything you need to live a quiet and peaceful life. You won't find a busy nightlife in Viseu, but if you are a wine lover, you will be happy to know that winemaking is a deep-rooted tradition here.

## SOUTH OF PORTUGAL
*"Sul De Portugal"*

### THE ALGARVE: THE FLORIDA OF EUROPE

*"Algarve: A Florida De Europe"*

- The Algarve region is a few hours away by car or train from Lisbon. Translated as the "West," a mountain chain separates it from the rest of Portugal. As you move inland, you will be met with a dry landscape with sparse inhabitants, many being retirees.

- It has around 400.000 inhabitants, mainly living in Faro (the capital and the largest city and least touristy place and home to an international airport), Albufeira (the party city known for its nightlife), and Portimão (the shopping center).

- Lagos is more family oriented but is located further west, an hour and a half from Faro. Tavira is one of the best and most beautiful places to stay in the Algarve. It's quieter, more relaxed, and only two hours from Seville, Spain. But if you want to live close to the beach and like shopping, Praia da Rocha is one of the largest and most popular beach resort towns on the Algarve.

- You will experience over 300 days of sunshine living in the Algarve. The World Travel Awards gave the Algarve region the title of "the World's Leading Beach Destination" in 2021. Also known as the "Oscar" of the Tourism Awards, it is the most important tourism award on the planet, and that is because the Algarve has some of the safest and cleanest beaches in the world.

- Traffic in the Algarve is low compared to Lisbon. However, because public transportation needs to be better developed, most people travel by car, which often ends up causing traffic on the main route, the EN125, with everyone trying to avoid the road tolls.

**Note:** The Algarve is a great region for retirement.

WHY THE ALGARVE
*"Porque Escolher O Algarve"*

Unlike the Azores, you can rent or own a car to travel to places all over Europe without the hassle of getting to an airport. The quality of life is excellent, especially if you don't have to commute to work. It's a sunny region with the most beautiful beaches in Portugal and popular with ex-pats; it is also home to a prominent British community.

WHY NOT THE ALGARVE
*"Porque Não Escolher O Algarve"*

You won't have the same variety of products you have in Lisbon, for example, which will translate to higher prices for some imported items, and you will have less access to cultural programs compared to the rest of the country. It being popular with ex-pats can be a downside because it can be expensive and not necessarily the lifestyle you want.

*Serra Da Estrela, Covilhá, Portugal*

## ALENTEJO: THE HEART OF PORTUGAL

*"Alentejo: O Caraçáo De Portugal"*

- The Alentejo region is a rural area with some of the most beautiful coastal zones with the lowest population density in Portugal. It covers a large part of the country and is one of the less expensive areas of the entire countryside, to the point of having most of its main cities listed as some of the cheapest cities to live in Portugal. The climate is good overall, with burning dry summers inland and cold rainy winters. The weather is less extreme on the coastal side.

- The Alentejo comprises five districts named after their capital cities: Santarém, Portalegre, Évora, Setúbal (located in the southern part of the district), and Beja. Évora, the capital, is 130km or 82 mi away from Lisbon and one of the most important cities in the Alentejo region. It could be a great place to live if you're looking for a peaceful lifestyle, not isolated but far enough from the big crowds. It is a fantastic city for students and ex-pats because it holds a university that accepts international students and has one of the largest public hospitals in Alejento.

- And as the new Golden Visa rules favor the Alentejo real estate market, more foreigners have discovered this Portugal hidden gem. For example, Santarém has been attracting Digital Nomads and new businesses because you can enjoy a quiet life while working remotely. The downside is that not every place has good internet coverage.

- In 2019, Forbes magazine described the Alentejo as 'the new place to go in Portugal," with the Alentejo

197

Coast attracting rich celebrities like George Clooney and Christian Louboutin and affluent Lisbon families.

## WHY NOT THE ALEJENTO REGION
*"Porque Não Escolher O Território De Alejento"*

Unfortunately, the public healthcare reputation could be better in the Alejento region. The lack of specialized doctors and long waiting periods are common, so private health care is highly recommended. And it may take longer to get to a hospital if you live in a remote area in the Alentejo region.

## WHY CHOOSE THE ALEJENTO REGION
*"Porque Escolher O Território De Alejento"*

If you value privacy and tranquility and like to be close to nature, this is the place for you. And like the rest of Portugal, the cost of living is low.

## CASCAIS

Cascais is still considered a village, despite its importance in terms of inhabitants and despite being home to the wealthy. That is because it is a small fishing community. You can drive to Sintra in 15-20 minutes because Cascais is about 20 miles or 32 km away from Lisbon or 40 minutes by train. If you have children, Cascais should definitively be your first choice because of the size of the ex-pat community; 16% of the population in Cascais are foreigners, which means more choices of schools. And since it has good weather, your children will spend more time playing outside.

## LISBON

### *"Lisboa"*

As Portugal's capital city, Lisbon is a mix of old buildings, castles, restaurants, hills, streetcars, narrow streets, and lots of traffic. Most of the city was wiped out by an earthquake known as the Great Lisbon Earthquake in 1755, but you wouldn't know that given that all of it has been practically rebuilt.

The food is excellent, the people friendly and the weather can be gloomy because the Atlantic brings a lot of rain. Winters are mild, and summers are hot, thanks to its subtropical-Mediterranean climate, making Lisbon one of the warmest capital cities in Europe.

It is more cosmopolitan and multicultural than other Portuguese cities and by far the most crowded city in the country because, besides the locals, everyone else lives here; tourists, students, nomads, and ex-pats. You can easily navigate life in Lisbon if you only speak English or French, as long as you avoid speaking Spanish.

#### PROS OF LIVING IN LISBON
*"Vantagens De Viver Em Lisboa"*

Like any big city, you can walk anywhere or take the subway. The other advantage of living in Lisbon is easy access to the best hospitals. You also have more schools to choose from, and there is an international airport.

CONS OF LIVING IN LISBON
*"Desvantagens De Viver Em Lisboa"*

Like Porto, Lisbon is no longer part of the Portugal Golden Visa Program. Driving and parking in Lisbon are messy, and public parking is expensive.

## SINTRA

Sintra is a must-see when visiting Lisbon. It is an affluent neighborhood on the Portuguese Riviera, less than 40 minutes away from Lisbon by train. It is also part of the Lisbon - Sintra - Cascais triangle. It is a beautiful area of forest, steep hills, villas, and mansions. If you don't live in Sintra, you can still go there for sightseeing or a walk in the woods.

CONS OF LIVING IN SINTRA
*"Desvantagens De Viver Em Sintra"*

Like Porto and Lisbon, Sintra is no longer eligible for the Golden Visa Residential Real Estate Investment. It is also one of Lisbon's most expensive, overpopulated, and touristy villages, making traffic a nightmare. It has no beaches since it is inland, but the ocean is pretty close. If you are not willing to live in a place that requires some driving to get to the beach, then Cascais might be the answer.

## MADEIRA ISLAND
## THE PEARL OF THE ATLANTIC - THE HAWAII OF EUROPE

*Madeira, Portugal*

If you are planning to retire in Portugal with the Golden Visa program or are a Digital Nomad seeking to settle in Portugal, Madeira might be the answer for you. This autonomous region is far south of Portugal, and like the Azores, it has a Hawaiian feel. It is home to Cristiano Ronaldo (CR7), who was born in Funchal, the capital. This is important because Cristiano Ronaldo is the pride of the Portuguese soccer team, if not of the whole country.

Porto Santo is its second smaller island and is easily accessible from Funchal by plane or boat. It is where Christopher Columbus lived because that's where his wife was from (their house is still there).

You will find two main types of ex-pat communities in Madeira, the traditional ex-pat community of retirees, mainly from the UK and Germany, and the more diverse new ex-pat community of Remote Workers and Digital Nomads from all over the world.

The project "Digital Nomad Village of Madeira" has helped put Madeira on the map by generating a lot of buzz around the island. So, if you move to Madeira, you will find a whole infrastructure to help you settle. There are many Digital Nomad/International Networking Events all over the island. They can be found in Funchal, where most ex-pats live, or Ponta do Sol, Calheta, and Caniço.

Though much of the island is hilly, there are plenty of walkable areas near the sea. Downtown Funchal, Ponta do Sol, the Lido area, Praia Formosa, Câmara do Lobos, and Caniço de Baixo are all walkable.

> **Note**: If walking is a problem for you, you should get a car or stay close to the sea because it's almost impossible to walk in some areas as the hills are too steep.

It takes approximately 1 hour and 30 minutes to fly from Madeira to Lisbon. If you fear flying, maybe you should know that Funchal's airport was once considered one of the world's most dangerous. Currently, three airlines fly daily between Madeira and mainland Portugal: TAP Air Portugal, EasyJet, and, most recently, Ryanair.

Some parts of the island are cooler than others. Still, the two top destinations, Funchal and Ponta do Sol, are usually warm, the latter being the sunniest spot on the island, with great potential for buying and renovating properties. Know that the north side of the island has even more affordable properties.

Like the rest of the country, Madeira is safe, with low rates of all types of crimes, such as pickpocketing and stealing, and is accepting of LGBTQ residents.

CONS OF LIVING IN MADEIRA
*"Desvantagens De Viver Em Madeira"*

The airport literally sits at the bottom of a carved mountainside with the Atlantic all around. You can find videos on YouTube of planes landing at Funchal's airport. It's pretty impressive. And unfortunately, flying will be your only means of traveling which is not ideal if you have aerophobia. And if you are claustrophobic, living on an island might not help, not to mention loneliness.

Madeiran locals only buy below the "Banana Line," which is not more than 200-300 meters above sea level. In fact, the island rises about 6km from the bed of the Atlantic Ocean, so properties above a certain altitude are more likely to have mold problems.

And some parts of the island – mainly on the east coast – are prone to high winds, especially during winter, which can damage properties not built to withstand them.

PROS OF LIVING IN MADEIRA
*"Vantagens De Viver Em Madeira"*

If you ever dreamed of living in Hawaii, try Madeira. You will be living on an island in Europe, surrounded by other nomads, which means the chances for you to feel alone will be low. For anyone looking to invest in Portugal, Madeira is a great investment opportunity. And if that was not enough, this is also where two of the most famous men of their times lived: Cristopher Columbus and Cristiano Ronaldo.

## ONE LAST WORD
*"Uma Última Palavra"*

If you enjoyed this book, help other readers by leaving a review on Amazon. Follow this link. Thank you!

https://www.amazon.com/review/create-review/?channel=glance-detail&asin=B0BZTQ9GWB&ie=UTF8

The world is full of beautiful places to explore, and for me Portugal is one of them. If you dream of a safer, freer, and more affordable life and the country calls you, book a trip and go experience the sights, sounds, fragrances, culture, food, and people. If Portugal turns out not to be the right fit for you, keep exploring. While Germany has a Freelancer's Visa, check out the many other European countries, such as Italy and Greece, that have Digital Nomad Visas. If Europe is too cold for you, try Bali. With so many countries offering Nomad Visas, the possibilities are endless. The goal is to start somewhere; let Portugal be that starting point.

And before you put the book down, turn the page and quiz yourself about Portugal!

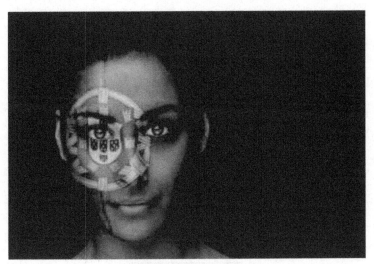

*Portugal Soccer Fan*

*"The future belongs to those who believe in the beauty of their dreams."*

- Eleanor Roosevelt

# TEST YOUR KNOWLEDGE

"TESTE SEU CONHECIMENTO"

Have fun answering the questions, then check your answers.

1 What is the capital of Portugal?

2 Is Portugal in Europe or the European Union?

3 Among these low-value products, which one Portugal produces the most? Textile, Cork, or Cosmetics?

4 How do you say Mister in Portuguese? Señor or Senhor?

5 What is the Iberian Peninsula?

6 What country does Portugal share borders with? France, Morocco, or Spain?

7 What do you call the inhabitants of Lisbon? "Lisboetas" or "Alfacinhas"?

8 People of Portuguese descent or origin are called Lusitanos. Y/N

9 Do you need to be a resident or have a visa to buy a car in Portugal?

10 Who is Portugal's number-one soccer player? Cristiano Ronaldo, Ronaldinho, or Ronaldo?

11 How do you say, "Do you speak Portuguese?" in Portuguese? "Falas português?" "Hablas portugues?" or "Parlas portugues?"

12 Portuguese is the official language of how many countries? How many can you name?

13 Are "Padarias" bakeries or pastries?

14 Fado means fade in Portuguese. Y/N

15 There are four types of visas: Tourist, Immigration, Student, and Work Visas. Those four types of visas can all fall under which three categories? Premium Stay, Short Stay, Temporary Stay, or Long Stay?

16 A visa-free entry allows you to enter Portugal for free. Y/N

17 Are all countries in Europe members of the Schengen Area? Y/N

18 What is a WWOOFer?

19 All Long-Term or Residence visas can lead to Portuguese Citizenship. Y/N

20 What is the difference between residence visas and residence permits?

21 Is an Eu-Blu Card a type of visa, a credit card, or an ID card?

22 Can you get your NIF online? Y/N?

23 What is a digital nomad?

24 Who can apply for the D7 Visa?

25 Can anyone apply for a D2 visa? Y/N

26 What is the Portugal Digital Nomad Visa also called?

27 How much money do you need to qualify for the Portugal Digital Nomad Visa?

28  Are D7 visas and the Portugal Digital Nomad Visas the same?

29  Which cities are no longer eligible for the Golden Visa?

30  How is the process to get your Work Visa done?

31  Younger children must attend preschool in Portugal. Y/N

32  What is an "utente"?

33  What is a NIF used for?

34  You can book your SEF appointment by phone or online. Y/N

35  Who can benefit from Portugal's NHR (Non-Habitual Resident) Tax System?

36  What would you use the number 112 for in Portugal or other European countries?

37  You can drive with your country-issued driver's license in Portugal.

38  You can use gas, solar panels, or electricity for central heating in Portugal. Y/N

39  If you buy land in Portugal, you can build on it. Y/N

40  Porto and Lisbon are in the southern part of Portugal. Y/N

41  What is Porto famous for?

42  Where was Cristiano Ronaldo born?

43  On which big Portuguese island can you still buy property as part of the Portugal Golden Visa Scheme?

# ANSWERS

1  This is an easy one, Lisbon or Lisboa.

2  Both. Portugal is in Europe's continent and a member of the European Union, the political and economic union of 27 European member states.

3  "Cork." Most cork forests are in Portugal, making it the biggest cork manufacturer in the world. Cork oaks are harvested every nine years once they reach maturity. The harvest year is marked on the trunk, so each tree isn't harvested at the wrong time.

4  "Senhor." To not be mistaken for "Señor," the Spanish word for sir/mister.

5  A mountainous region that comprises Spain and Portugal (and a small area of Southern France, Andorra, and Gibraltar).

6  "Spain." Portugal shares a border with only Spain. The flight to Paris from Lisbon is 2h30 versus 1h20 from Lisbon to Morocco.

7  "The inhabitants of Lisbon are called both "Lisboetas" and "Alfacinhas.""

8  "People of Portuguese descent or origin are called "Lusitano/a." Lusitania is sometimes used as an alternative name for Portugal."

9   "You don't need a visa or be a resident to buy a car in Portugal."

10  "Cristiano Ronaldo is Portugal's number-one football/soccer player."

11  "Do you speak Portuguese?" is "Falas português?"

12  Portuguese is the official language of Brazil, Cape Verde, Angola, Guinea Bissau, Mozambique, Principe, Sao Tome, and Equatorial Guinea.

13  "Padarias" are bakeries. They sell mainly bread and cakes, and it is common for Portuguese people to have breakfast at these places. "Pastelarias" are pastry shops that sell cakes, pastries, and sweets/candies.

14  One of Portugal's national treasures and music pride is Fado.

15  There are four types of visas: Tourist, Immigration, Student, and Work Visas. Those four types of visas can all fall under these three categories: Short Stay, Temporary Stay, and Long Stay Visas, depending on their length and purposes.

16  If you are a US citizen or are from a country with visa-free agreements with Portugal, you won't need a visa to travel to Portugal and the other Schengen Member States for up to 90 days.

17  There are 44 countries in Europe, and only 27 are state members of the European Union. Iceland, Liechtenstein, and Norway are not part of the EU but are part of the Single Market Trade (the free movement of goods and people in the EU that allows

people to work, shop, travel, study, and retire anywhere in the EU).

18 "Worldwide Opportunities on Organic Farms" is a network that links volunteers to organic farms, where they work on the farm in exchange for food and accommodation.

19 Yes, all Long-Term or Residence Visas can lead to Portuguese Citizenship.

20 Residence Visas differ from Residence Permits. A residence visa gives you the right to travel to Portugal, while a residence permit is a document that allows you to stay long-term in Portugal.

21 An Eu-Blu Card is a visa for highly skilled people.

22 The answer is yes; you can get your NIF online.

23 A digital nomad chooses to work remotely in a country that is not his and relies on their computer to access their job.

24 The D7 Visa is for self-employed, freelancers, or remote workers who want to establish themselves in Portugal.

25 The D2 visa is for non-EU/EEA or Swiss citizens who want to start a new business in Portugal.

26 The Portugal Digital Nomad Visa is also called the Remote Work Visa.

27 The minimum monthly income for the Portugal Digital Nomad Visa must be at least four times the Portuguese minimum wage per month.

28 Though they are both nomad visas, anyone can apply for a D7 visa, while the Portugal Digital Nomad visa is meant explicitly for remote workers.

29 Since January 2022, you can no longer purchase real estate in Lisbon (which includes Sintra, Cascais, the Algarve, etc.), Porto, and the coastal towns to obtain a Portugal Golden Visa.

30 The process to get your Work Visa is done in two times. Your Employer will first apply for a Work Permit on your behalf from the Portuguese Labor Authorities, and only then will you be able to apply for a Work Visa.

31 Attending Preschool "Jardim de Infância" is not mandatory in Portugal. However, Ensino Basico is mandatory, while Ensino Secundario is optional.

32 NIF, the Portuguese Tax Number, or "Número de Identificação Fiscal," is a unique nine-digit number issued to each person. It will appear on your tax and Portuguese citizenship identity cards and is needed to deal with many transactions in the country, from getting your phone subscription, buying property, renting property long-term, signing up for utilities, and getting your residency permit, to paying your taxes, enrolling at a school, opening bank accounts, and so on.

33 The SEF Customer Service Bureau has a pre-booking system that allows you to book, cancel or reschedule your appointment by phone or online.

34 You'll need a unique identifying number (Utente) to access public healthcare in Portugal. You can apply for your SNS number once you officially get your residence permit in Portugal.

35 You will fall under the NHR (Non-Habitual Resident) tax system if you have a Golden Visa, a D7 Visa, and a D2 Visa.

36 112 is Europe's Medical Emergency Number and is free of charge, 24/7.

37 No. You can drive in Portugal with your country-issued driver's license for a period that should be at most 185 days if you are not a legal resident.

38 Gas, solar panels, or electricity can all be used for central heating.

39 Before purchasing land in Portugal, it is crucial to make sure that you can build on it.

40 Only Lisbon and Sintra are in the south of Portugal.

41 Porto is famous for the Porto wine, the "Tripas à Moda do Porto," and its football/soccer club: F.C. Porto.

42 Cristiano Ronaldo was born in Funchal, the capital of Madeira.

43 Madeira.

# ACKNOWLEDGEMENTS

## "RECONHECIMENTOS"

https://buyproperty.com

https://www.expatica.com/pt/moving/visas/golden-visa-portugal-1042263/

https://www.expatica.com/pt/moving/about/cost-of-living-in-portugal-1167462/

https://www.internationalinsurance.com/hospitals/portugal/

https://viveurope.com

https://www.portugal.com/travel/portugal-d2-visa-portugals-entrepreneur-visa/

https://www.portugal.com/travel/portugal-golden-visa-the-ultimate-guide-to-portugals-golden-visa/

https://www.crownportugal.eu

https://visaguide.world

www.investopedia.com

https://www.seg-social.pt/inicio

https://schengen.europ-assistance.com/en/what-are-different-types-schengen-visas

https://www.study-research.pt/

https://beportugal.com

https://www.facebook.com/groups/portugalpropertyunder100k/?ref=share

https://www.schengenvisainfo.com

https://www.atlys.com

https://digitalemigre.com

https://vistos.mne.gov.pt/en

https://www.angloinfo.com

https://www.expatarrivals.com

https://immigrantinvest.com

https://www.portugalhomes.com/

https://beportugal.com/braganca-portugal/

https://porto-north-portugal.com

https://internationalliving.com

https://portugaltravelguide.com/where_to_go/azores/

https://www.international-schools-database.com/in/lisbon/the-british-school-lisbon/fees

https://thesologlobetrotter.com/portugal-quotes-about-portugal/

https://www.portugal-the-simple-life.com/post/car-ownership-driving

https://getgoldenvisa.com/silver-coast-portugal#ftoc-where-to-live-in-portugal-silver-

https://www.portugalist.com/buying-property-Portugal/

https://www.cnbc.com

https://www.washingtonpost.com

https://outandbeyond.com

https://www.mbopartners.com

https://thinkremote.com

https://www.practiceportuguese.com

https://joyofmuseums.com

https://ai.glossika.com

https://www.thetravellingtom.com/

https://www.jcjourneys.com

https://visaguide.world/golden-visa/

https://boundlesshq.com/guides/portugal/benefits/

https://viveurope.com/living-in-alentejo/

https://www.dges.gov.pt/

https://www.dreambigtravelfarblog.com/blog/digital-nomad-statistics

https://www.forbes.com/sites/ceciliarodriguez/2023/02/17/portugal-ends-golden-visa-program-after-ireland-and-before-spain/?sh=e26927e66cae

Made in United States
Orlando, FL
06 November 2024